The Birth of Oakalla
Pre-1912

Alec "The Skunk" Ignace had earned his nickname. Born and raised on the Kamloops Reservation, the twenty-five-year-old Native Indian had a nasty reputation for being out of control when he was drunk. His outbursts became so terrifying that his wife Minnie left him and took shelter with another family. Ignace was deeply embarrassed by this, and after several months of festering resentment, he could see only one way to end his hatred towards her. On the chilly afternoon of January 7, 1919, Ignace grabbed his gun, washed back a few drinks of hard liquor, and saddled his horse.

Shortly before 3:00 p.m. he arrived at a bend in the gravel road which ran between Schiedam and the Reserve. After a few minutes, an old Democrat rumbled around the corner. Ignace hid out of view until the car passed, then started out after it. He quickly gained on the slow moving vehicle and its four occupants. In the back seat, behind the driver, he spotted his target. Keeping his horse parallel with the car, Ignace reached down to the saddle and pulled a .30 calibre U.S. army rifle from its sheath. As the weapon was being raised, Minnie looked over her shoulder and let out a scream as she recognized

7

her husband. The driver attempted to swerve as the rifle let out a thundering blast, but the soft-nosed bullet exploded from the muzzle and ripped into Minnie's abdomen.

Without a word Ignace turned and galloped away, heading towards the river bank, then north past Seven Mile camp, and into the eastern hills. Minnie slumped over on the seat, bleeding profusely. She was dead within minutes. Her horrified companions quickly drove to Kamloops, where they notified the Provincial Police. By 4:30 p.m. Chief Constable Adam and Constable McLeod had organized a posse of Indian trackers.

While news of the murder spread, Ignace spent the night hiding in the safety of the local mountains. At daybreak he spotted the trackers as they passed through Seven Mile camp and contemplated trying to pick them off with his rifle as they made their way along the trails. Instead, he opted to flee south and head towards the United States, but first he had to stop at home and pick up some clothing and extra food.

Before leaving on the manhunt, Chief Adam speculated that the felon might return and stationed three special Indian constables to watch his residence. When Ignace returned to his shack, the police were waiting, and arrested him without incident. Ignace was taken to the Kamloops Provincial Gaol. The following day, satisfied there was enough evidence to proceed with a trial, Magistrate Fisher ordered him remanded at the newly constructed, maximum-security Oakalla Prison Farm.

The trial was scheduled for May, and after three months of incarceration in the West Wing, Ignace read the writing on the wall. He would likely be found guilty and sentenced to death. Determined not to meet the hangman and his noose, he started planning an escape. On the afternoon of March 25, two bars covering a window at the end of a tier were sawn through with a secreted table knife. Thirteen prisoners stood by "keeping six" as Ignace, George "Scotty" Stone, imprisoned on burglary charges, and bank robber Walter Martin climbed through the window, slid down a rope made of sheets, and scrambled over a fence into the heavily wooded area near Royal Oak Avenue.[1] Fate was not in "The Skunk's" favour, however. Early the following day, he and the other escapees were apprehended by a contingent of police and guards who had scoured the countryside.

Found guilty of first-degree murder on May 16, Ignace was scheduled to hang on the fourth of July. In early June, there was a reprieve, a faint glimmer of hope, as counsel tried for a commutation of sentence. It ended fruitlessly. When the appeal failed he was taken from the West Wing to a special holding cell built on the bottom floor of the wooden Old Gaol. Except for a guard watching over him twenty-four hours a day, he was alone.

Several days before Ignace was scheduled to die, carpenters assembled a wooden scaffold in the prison courtyard. Thirteen steps led from the ground to the platform, where a four-by-four foot trap door was cut out in the middle, and straddled by a sturdy wooden beam. The gallows were designed to be easily dismantled and reassembled when the occasion arose. The day before the hanging, Arthur Ellis, Canada's official executioner, arrived at Oakalla and had the prisoner measured and weighed. He was five-foot-five, and weighed 130 pounds. The hangman measured some rope and tied it off at the appropriate length. He then tested the gallows using a bag of sand equal to the prisoner's weight.

On the following morning, as the sun was beginning to rise, a Catholic priest stood outside Ignace's cell and asked the prisoner to join him in a prayer. Arthur Ellis and two guards then entered the cell and bound the prisoner's hands behind his back. Ignace was brought into the courtyard of the Old Gaol. In addition to Warden Campbell and his staff, about twenty-five civilians and a few members of the press were in attendance, at the invitation of the Sheriff of New Westminster.

Once the prisoner and his escorts reached the platform, Ellis bound Ignace's legs together with rope, then put the noose over Ignace's head so that it rested around his neck. After placing a black cloth hood over the prisoner's head, Ellis motioned to the priest, who began to recite the Lord's Prayer: "Our Father, which art in Heaven..." The Warden and the crowd of onlookers had all joined in the familiar verse by the time he had finished. There was a moment of silence. Seconds later the stillness was broken by the crash of the trap doors falling open. The body plunged downward and the rope went taut.

The small crowd of onlookers appeared repulsed as they watched the body awkwardly twist and squirm for several agonizing seconds before all movement finally ceased. It wasn't an instantaneous death. After several minutes, the attending physician ordered the body cut down. At 7:40 a.m. he declared the prisoner dead and signed the Certificate of Execution, which was then posted at the front gate, for all to witness that justice had been served. It was August 29, 1919. Alec Ignace was the first of many prisoners to sit on Oakalla's Death Row, and the first of forty-four official executions carried out within its walls (see Appendix A).

Sensational events such as this were repeated many times over the

9

course of the prison's life, and before long Oakalla had gained a reputation as both a punishing yet relatively easily escapable institution. However, less than a decade earlier, Oakalla's blueprints had not even been drawn. The need to build a large provincial prison, in the heart of the Lower Mainland, arose at the turn of the century, when severe overcrowding and dilapidation of the Common Gaol at New Westminster reached a critical state.

When British Columbia joined Confederation in 1871, one of the promises made by the federal government to the financially strapped province was to build immediately a penitentiary for inmates serving sentences of two years or more. The province would remain accountable for those convicted of less serious crimes. At the time, all British Columbia offenders had to be committed to one of the three gaols (New Westminster, Kamloops, or Victoria), regardless of the length of sentence. However by the late 1800s the rapid increase in the population, and a corresponding surge in crime, had virtually overflowed the capacities of the Victoria and New Westminster prisons. When the British Columbia Penitentiary opened in September 1887, it absorbed only twenty-three convicts, which did little to ease overcrowding.

Following the arrival of the first transcontinental CPR train in 1887, not only did Vancouver's economy and population boom, so did its crime rate. This was especially evident with the illicit opium drug trade, which flourished because of Vancouver's accessibility to Asia, where it was grown, and easy distribution across Canada and the United States using legitimate transportation routes.

Two decades later, a worldwide economic depression hit Vancouver hard as labourers throughout the province migrated to the Lower Mainland, hoping to find work in the big city. This was compounded by the large number of unemployed who moved to the mild West Coast from the Prairie Provinces and Eastern Canada to escape bitter winters. The local police found themselves charging an ever-increasing number of citizens with minor thefts, assaults, and vagrancy. The courts, in turn, were sending more and more people to prison. The problem was that the New Westminster Provincial Gaol had to serve the entire Lower Mainland.

By 1911, all seventy-seven cells of the twenty-six year-old prison were always full. A Grand Jury had also recently inspected the facility and found it to be poorly ventilated and a major fire hazard. The Jury recommended that a new prison be built in the area to replace the gaol.

Several months later, the provincial government announced that a new, centrally-located prison farm would be built in Burnaby to serve the Lower Mainland. It would be large enough to hold several hundred sentenced prisoners, plus those held in custody while awaiting trial or transfer to the federal penitentiary. Since the prison was to be run as a farm, it would require significant acreage, so that all inmate labour could be conducted within the perimeter of the prison property. This would eliminate the need for Chain Gangs, which had proven to be high escape risks.

On May 23, 1911, the Provincial Department of Public Works issued a call for tenders for the erection of a prison farm on Burnaby's District Lot 84, Group 1. The wooded 185 acre site sloped down towards the south-west side of Deer Lake. It offered a breathtaking view of the open meadows around the lake, with the snow-capped North Shore mountains in the far distance. On the west side of the property was Royal Oak Road, which climbed straight up a steep bumpy hill and, at the top, intersected with Vancouver Road (Kingsway), the main transportation route linking New Westminster and Vancouver.

At the time, Burnaby's population was dramatically rising, doubling in just two years, and now topped 10,000. Still, there were few residents surrounding Lot 84; most of them being fruit and vegetable farmers. However, the north and east shores of Deer Lake had recently become prime real estate for Vancouver's wealthier citizens desiring a country setting. For example, two years earlier, *Fairacres,* a mansion unrivaled in the city for its opulence, had been built on the north side of the lake. When these residents learned of the plan to build a prison in their neighbourhood they launched a protest. The Burnaby Board of Trade forwarded a letter to the provincial government which appeared in the July 24, 1911 issue of the *British Columbia Gazette:*

> That this board forward a respectful protest to the provincial government against the establishment of a prison farm on D.L. 84, in the midst of the best residential location in Burnaby, upon the grounds (1), of its being detrimental to the district; and (2) the occupation of a site worth in the market over $300,000, while the government possesses other lands, 160 acres in extent, in Burnaby, worth only $95,000.[2]

The government made a small concession to the community's residents by setting aside a parcel of land skirting the south-west side of the lake for the local Parks Commission.

Architect Hugh A. Hodgson designed the prison in a cross formation, facing northeast, so that "all cells would get sunshine at some time of the day." "It was to be both structurally and in equipment thoroughly up-to-date, having been carefully planned with a view to obtaining perfect light, ventilation and sanitation, in conjunction with absolute security."[3]

On October 9, 1911, Messrs. Smith and Sherborne of Vancouver were awarded the contract to construct the facility, at an estimated cost of $267,000. Partly because the country was in the midst of a depression, racist organizations, such as the Asiatic Exclusion League, were able to convince politicians that minority immigrants were scooping up precious jobs, because they were willing to work for virtually slave-labour wages. The provincial government conceded to their pressure and included the following restriction in the contract:

> The Contractor shall not, directly or indirectly, employ
> Chinese, Japanese, or any other Asiatics upon, about,
> or in connection with the works; and in the event of
> his so doing, the Government will not be responsible
> for payment of his Contract.[4]

More than seventy-five local men were hired and slept in temporary bunkhouses during the three years of construction. Tons of brick and other materials were required to build Oakalla and a spur line of the B.C. Electric Railway was built from Royal Oak Station, down the hill, to the front of the Main Gaol. Only six months after the project began it became apparent that the New Westminster Gaol could no longer continue to hold all its prisoners. As a result, it was announced that a temporary gaol would be built, which would be ready for occupancy in half a year.

The wooden temporary gaol, capable of housing more than 100 prisoners, consisted of three buildings assembled in a horseshoe pattern with a concrete wall on the fourth side; creating a central quadrangle. This open area was the prisoners' exercise yard, and the location of the Ignace and other outdoor hangings. In the basement of the North Wing were dungeon-like Dark Cells and, on the top floor, living quarters for six officers.

When the cross-shaped Main Gaol was completed in 1914, it was 346 feet by 195 feet. The outer walls were of red Clayburn bricks, five layers deep, and reinforced with steel bands. The East and West Wings each contained 160 regular cells, plus six punishment cells. The smaller South Wing was built for women, and had accommodation for just fifty-four prisoners. All cells, save those for punishment, contained a cold water basin, a toilet, a metal-framed bed hinged to the side wall, and an inspection slot in the rear wall.

A spur line was built in 1911 to bring materials to Oakalla's construction site

Before admitting its first inmate, the gaol had been referred to by many names, but not "Oakalla." The name originated from the district of Burnaby in which the prison was located. On August 1, 1912, a post office was opened near Royal Oak Avenue and Kingsway. Area residents wanted to name it the "Royal Oak" Post Office; however, there was already one bearing that name on Vancouver Island. Rather than lose the identity of their area, they named it the "Oakalla" Post Office: "alla" comes from the last two letters of Royal, and then reversed.[5] When the prison opened it was officially titled "Prison Farm, Oakalla, B.C." Later, it became known as "Oakalla Prison Farm," or simply "Oakalla."

Oakalla reflected the American "Auburn" model of penology: inmates would be subjected to harsh discipline and strenuous work during the day, and segregated in individual cells at night.[6] It was believed that these controls, strictly enforced, would bring about the reform of every offender. Oakalla was to bring penal practices in British Columbia into a new era. The new prison would also allow exhausted institutions to close their doors. In 1912, the provincial government saw Oakalla as a godsend to corrections. In the years that followed, it was more often considered the devil's work.

Legend

1. Main Gaol (1914);
2. Old Gaol (1912);
3. Cow Barns;
4. Women's Prison -Lakeside - (1940);
5. Gatehouse;
6. Warden's Residence;
7. Gymnasium (1955);
8. Westgate (1952);
9. Young Offenders' Unit (1951)/
   Health Care Centre(1962).

Two

The Early Years
1912-1929

In the summer of 1912, there was no hoopla or fanfare as the government prepared to open the gates to British Columbia's largest provincial institution. The administration of prisons was the responsibility of the B.C. Provincial Police, and Superintendent William G. McMynn was chosen to be Oakalla's first warden. He brought with him a handful of former policemen to work and live at the gaol, and operate it in strict military fashion.

Thirty-two-year-old William Daley was Oakalla's first inmate. On July 31, 1912, he was apprehended on the streets of Vancouver for stealing fountain pens worth more than ten dollars. Two weeks later, he pleaded guilty to the charge and was sentenced to one year's hard labour, to be served at the Common Gaol, New Westminster. Colin Campbell, the new Superintendent of Provincial Police, advised Warden McMynn on August 29, that he would be transferring Daley to Oakalla, primarily because he was reported to be a "good cook." On September 1, the slightly-built petty thief arrived at Oakalla under police escort.

The following day, twenty-three more felons were brought to

Oakalla's First Warden, William G. McMynn.

Oakalla from the New Westminster Gaol. Within a few months, some semblance of a functioning prison began to unfold. Prisoners sentenced in the Lower Mainland, those serving sentences longer than six months, and higher security-risk prisoners were all brought to the new prison.

Daley must have been a good cook. When he was discharged, on June 10, 1913, he was handed $27.00, "on behalf of the officers of the Prison Farm with their best wishes." A guard's monthly salary was only $85.00.

Within a year, Oakalla's inmate count rose to more than 200, and the overcrowding crisis in B.C.'s prisons was eliminated. The gaol was also designed to bring the treatment of offenders into a new era of penology. Convicts were to be reformed and educated through hard work and learning new labour skills, instead of having to endure long hours of isolation which had typified earlier institutions. Before 1914, much of the labour for the first inmates consisted of assisting with the construction of their cells in the brick Main Gaol.

Local resident Bert Price remembered Oakalla's first prisoners. In 1910 his father had bought land near Deer Lake, on property which later became part of Oakalla:

> When the prison began to operate, the prisoners themselves cleared the land for more buildings with gun powder and horses; just like the settlers around them. There were no fences, and the people in the neighbourhood never locked their doors.
> A little two-by-four store run by a man named MacEdwards sold candy and cigarettes to the prisoners called trusties. Despite the lack of fences, there were few escapes. The prisoners always kept the place looking neat and tidy.[1]

In the early 1900s Oakalla was no different from any other North American prison or penitentiary. Silence was strictly enforced, inmates were sentenced to hard labour, and gaolers had complete control over their charges. Those sentenced to hard labour left for work by 7:30 a.m. (8:00 a.m. during winter months) and would not return from the fields or workshops until 5:30 p.m. Dressed in grey denim trousers, tunic, and cap, inmates would walk in unison to and from the fields. Clearly marked across the back of their jackets and along one side of their pants were the letters P G (Provincial Gaol) with a broad arrow between them. Their uniforms were easily distinguishable to the ever-present armed guards. The prisoners were locked in their cells

Inmates clearing land, circa 1914.

at 7:00 p.m. and lights-out was at 9:00 p.m.

For many years there was a two-scale diet system at the prison, one for inmates sentenced to hard labour, where the labour was "ordinary work inside the Gaol," and the second for prisoners whose labour consisted of "cutting wood and breaking stones, or any work necessitating the exercising of strength." These are the two diets as prescribed in Section 59 of the Rules and Regulations:

SCALE NO. 1.

Breakfast.

One pint of gruel (made from oatmeal or Indian-corn meal) and eight ounces of bread every morning.

Dinner.

Five ounces of cooked meat (without bone), eight

ounces of bread, and eight ounces of potatoes, on three days of the week. Eight ounces of bread, one pound of potatoes, and one pint of gruel, on two days in the week. One pint of soup and eight ounces of bread, on two days in the week.

Supper.

One pint of gruel and eight ounces of bread every night.

SCALE NO. 2.
Breakfast.

One pint of gruel, eight ounces of bread, and one pint of pea coffee sweetened with molasses, or brown sugar, every morning.

Dinner.

Six ounces of cooked meat (without bone), eight ounces of bread, and eight ounces of potatoes, on each day that hard labour is performed; otherwise Scale No. 1. to be followed.

Supper.

One pint of gruel and eight ounces of bread, every night.

Although Oakalla was to be more reformative than previous prisons by educating prisoners and teaching them labour skills, this did not imply that it was going to pamper them. The Gaol Rules and Regulations, revised on Oakalla's opening day, underlined how regimented daily life in prison was. These regulations were posted on every cell wall:

(1) The first duty of a prisoner is strict obedience;

(2) Strict silence must be observed in all parts of the Gaol. No conversation between prisoners will be allowed except by special permission of the Gaoler under whose charge they are;

(3) Prisoners shall rise at 6:30 o'clock a.m. from 1st April to 30th September, and at 7 o'clock a.m. from 1st October to 31st March, and will be allowed half an hour to wash, dress themselves, and clean their cells;

(4) Every prisoner shall sweep out his cell thoroughly upon getting up, empty the slop pail, and fold his bedding and leave it in a tidy state, and afterwards keep his cell and its contents in a neat and clean condition;

(5) Prisoners shall always approach all Gaol Officials in a respectful manner, speak in a respectful tone of voice, and in as few words as possible make their requests known;

(6) No prisoner shall possess himself of tobacco, matches, or any contraband article, instrument, or tool, no matter how small the size or quantity; and a prisoner found in possession of or attempting to smuggle any such thing into the Gaol will be dealt with as insubordinate;

(7) No prisoner shall mark or scratch the walls, spit on the floor, or deface, alter, or reconstruct any article or part of his bedding, dress, cell, or cell furniture, or waste, damage, or destroy any material upon which he is employed;

(8) No lights shall be allowed in any of the cells;

(9) Prisoners having any complaints to make may report them to the Warden, or to the Inspector during his inspections, who will investigate them, but a prisoner making complaints which he or she is unable to substantiate will be liable to be dealt with as insubordinate;

(10) Prisoners wishing to see and consult with their legal advisers or clergymen, or to converse with their friends, must apply to the Warden for permission to do so;

(11) No prisoner shall give anything to another prisoner;

(12) No local newspapers of any kind will be allowed to prisoners, and all other reading matter shall pass the Warden's inspection before it is given to prisoners;

(13) Prisoners sentenced to hard labour shall labour diligently during working hours;

(14) Every prisoner will find it to his interest at all times to conform to these Rules and to carefully read them over, but if a prisoner is unable to read, they will be read over and explained to him by an officer, on application, at a reasonable time.

The punishments for contravening these rules, set out in Section 46, were as follows:

(1) Solitary confinement in a dark cell, with or without bedding, not to exceed six days for any offence, nor three days at any one time;

(2) Bread and water diet, full or half rations, combined or not with No.(1)

Paulson and Robinson Hang

The Canadian Criminal Code, first enacted in 1869, was a mixture of English Common Law and existing Colonial laws based on the Judeo Christian ethic — a man is responsible and punishable for his crime. A central theme to punishment was retribution. If a man wilfully took another man's life, he must pay with his own. Oakalla now carried out all hangings in the province, assuming this authority from the New Westminster Provincial Gaol.

In April 1921, Alan Robinson and Alex Paulson, two petty criminals who made a specialty of hold-ups, shot and killed William Salsbury, son of a wealthy Canadian Pacific Railway executive during a bungled robbery attempt on Georgia Street in Vancouver. The pair spotted him walking alone one night and saw him as an easy target. However, when confronted, the popular oarsman lashed out at his attackers. Both men were carrying hand guns and a shot rang out. Salsbury dropped to the ground dead; a .32 calibre bullet had cut through his heart.

Painstaking investigation by Detective Grant of the Vancouver Police traced a torn piece of cloth, snagged on barbed wire near the scene, to a pair of pants that Alex Paulson had sold to a second-hand dealer. Six weeks later both men were in custody and pointing to each other as Salsbury's killer. At the trial both were initially found guilty and sentenced to hang. Later, Robinson was granted an appeal because he had testified for the Crown against Paulson. The judge at Robinson's second trial found insufficient evidence to consider clemency. The men then waited on Death Row for more than a year as their lawyer sought for reprieves to introduce new evidence. Time ran out for the men in July 1922, and an execution date was set for the 28th. In the last two hours before the scheduled 6:00 a.m. hanging, the pair's lawyer made a final plea to the Minister of Justice in Ottawa for another reprieve or commutation of sentence. Warden Colin Campbell had to temporarily postpone the hanging until he received a reply telegram from the capital stating that parliament would not interfere with the course of justice.[2]

Shortly after 8:00 a.m. the pair were taken into the courtyard and were bound together, back to back. They remained composed and silent throughout their final ordeal. Seconds later the trap doors opened and the two bodies plunged several feet until the ropes had reached the end of their lengths. The body of Robinson was sent to Eastern Canada, to be returned to his family, while Paulson's unclaimed remains were buried in a yard on prison grounds.[3] The latter statement is questionable. There is no record of Oakalla having its own burial grounds (although there was one at the B.C. Penitentiary), and there is no indication that remains were ever exhumed.

Baker and Myers

The most publicized hanging at Oakalla was that of Harry F. Myers (alias "Si" Sowash) and Owen B. "Cannonball" Baker on January 14, 1926. The arrest, trial, and execution of the pair were the subject of newspaper headlines for many months. Readers, both appalled and fascinated, followed the story to the end, to satisfy themselves that justice was meted out.

Prohibition began in the United States in 1920 and lasted until 1933. With the United States dry, and liquor in Canada flowing freely, it didn't take long for a major smuggling operation to emerge — and to make fortunes for underworld kingpins, such as Al Capone. The West Coast provided the perfect location for business between the neighbouring countries. The Gulf and San Juan Islands held hundreds of isolated coves and sheltered passages for rum-runners to dart in between, make trades, and lay caches of liquor, as they skirted the coast. At first, the smuggling trade was tolerated. Many of the authorities had been paid off, and they were willing to look the other way as these entrepreneurs went about their business. Then hijackers and pirates came on the scene. They would stop a vessel on its way down the coast, wave their guns around, and make off with their liquor. It was easy money — pure profit, and the victim was unlikely to report the robbery to the authorities. Soon the smugglers were carrying guns and it wasn't long before a captain was shot and wounded. After this incident, Canadian authorities took the matter seriously. They wanted to make an example out of someone, but they did not expect to contend with murder.

"Cannonball" Baker was a hijacker. He had recently served a three-year prison term for robbing a smuggler of his liquor on the streets of Tacoma. Those who knew him feared him. He boasted about his profession and seemed to have no fear himself. In September 1924 he called upon his business acquaintances Charlie Morris, Paul Stromkins, and Harry Sowash to pick up some liquor stashed around the Gulf Islands that his connections in the police department had told him about. They set out in Paul Stromkins' boat — the Denman II. The men never found their liquor, but Baker observed a boat pass him, which he knew would be carrying a cargo of liquid gold — the *Beryl G.*

William G. Gillis, skipper of the *Beryl G.*, and his 17-year-old son were relatively new to the liquor smuggling business, a middle-class Vancouver family, looking for a quick way to make a buck. On September 15, the *Beryl G.* met up with the steamship *Comet,* off the coast of Vancouver Island, and took on some 380 cases of whiskey and London Burnett Gin. They then sailed to Sidney Island, where they met with an American boat which was to take the alcohol down the coast to Tacoma. The American vessel was, however, much smaller than the *Beryl G.* and would have to make two runs. The men transferred 150 of the cases, and the remainder were to be picked up the following day at the same location. When the boat returned the following day, the *Beryl G.* was gone.

Late in the evening of September 13, Baker and his men left Victoria harbour in Stromkin's speedy gas boat and headed towards Sidney Island to intercept the *Beryl G.* Within two days the bandits had caught up with the liquor-laden vessel. When they were in close range, Baker, Morris, and Sowash boarded a skiff they had in tow and quietly approached the *Beryl G.* Baker carried a flashlight, handgun, and handcuffs. On the deck of the boat he called out that he was the law and ordered the crew out. Seconds later several shots rang out. Baker then ordered Stromkins to bring his boat up alongside. When Stromkins enquired about the shooting, Baker told him that he had to "shoot the old man a little in the arm."[4] The reality was that the captain had been shot to death. The son, however, was spared for a few hours. In the meantime, the men towed the *Beryl G.* to a small island and transferred the rum-runner's precious cargo. Once this was complete, Stromkins claimed that Sowash brought the youth out of the cabin and bludgeoned him to death.

Baker then prepared to dispose of the bodies. He took out his pair of handcuffs and clasped the father and son together. The ship's 150 pound anchor was then tied to the two bodies. Still not satisfied that the victims' remains would not be recovered, Baker took out his hunting knife and carved open the bellies of both men, ensuring himself that they would not float. The bodies were cast off the ship and the anchor was released when they were in open water. After their murderous journey, the felons returned to Sidney where they laid their large cache of the liquor in shallow water, hoping to pick it up later. All four then fled to various parts of the United States.

The tragedy was discovered several days later when the blood-splattered *Beryl G.* was found adrift. The bodies, however, were never recovered. Inspector Cruickshank and Sergeant Owens of the B.C. Provincial Police commenced their murder investigation by questioning known leaders of smuggling operations, and they soon discovered that a particular brand of gin which had recently turned up in Tacoma was the first shipment to arrive on the West Coast. The police believed that if they found other bottles of this gin, its distributor might know something about the *Beryl G.* The rest of the stash was located in

Victoria, and within days, the police had tracked down Stromkins, and took him in for questioning. He quickly fingered Baker and Sowash as the murderers. The local police contacted agencies throughout North America to be on the lookout for the suspects, and in less than a month, they had been apprehended—Baker in New York City, Sowash in New Orleans, and Morris in Seattle.

On the long train trip from New Orleans to Oakalla Prison, Sowash wrote a "confession" accusing Baker of murdering the two Gillis men. At Oakalla, he was reunited with Baker, Sowash, and Stromkins in the prison's West Wing. Morris was in Seattle, fighting extradition. Before the trial, prison guard John Delahunty intercepted a rolled-up magazine near Baker's cell. Between the pages was a copy of Sowash's confession and a corresponding list of instructions on how Baker could account for each paragraph.[5]

During the trial of Sowash and Baker, Stromkins was set free. His lawyer successfully argued that the accused's statements had been coerced from him. Instead of having to face the noose, he became the key witness for the prosecution. Sowash and Baker were convicted in June 1925 and sentenced to death. Their subsequent appeals also failed. Morris was later brought to Victoria, tried, convicted and sentenced to death. His appeal reduced the sentence to life imprisonment.

Throughout the many court appearances Sowash had refused to reveal his identity, stating that he had no living family or relatives. However, he was clearly intelligent and well educated. During the trial he would cover his face from the press, hoping to ensure that photos of himself would not reach his family. In his last months at Oakalla, some said that Sowash found religion. He became quite friendly with staff and fellow prisoners — but he still kept his identity a secret. On the night before he was to be hanged, he finally admitted to his minister that his surname was not Sowash but Myers, that he came from a wealthy American family, and that he had been married briefly. In the days before he was executed Myers wrote in his small journal a number of astute philosophical insights on correctional treatment and humanity. They were published the day of his execution on the front page of a local newspaper.

On January 14, 1926, the visitors' parking lot at Oakalla was filled to capacity. Security at the prison was stepped up: extra armed guards were called on duty to patrol the inside of the grounds; all witnesses were searched for weapons; and floodlights were mounted on the roof of the Main Gaol. Several years earlier, two well-known Canadian rum-runners attempted to escape custody in San Francisco before a trial. During the incident one of the escapees was accidentally shot and killed by an accomplice, but the other got away. Baker and Myers still had underworld connections and there was always the possibility of a last-minute breakout attempt.

The men walked to the gallows under guard at 7:30 a.m., and, as the morning rain fell, Baker casually puffed on a cigarette that was stuck in the corner of his mouth. Both men appeared relaxed; they said several good-byes, Baker took a few last drags of his smoke and then spat it out. The hangman placed the black hoods over their heads and there were a few more hurried muffled farewells to each other as Ellis made his last preparations. "Step on it kid! Make it fast!" Myers blurted out. Seconds later the executioner complied and pulled the lever.[6]

Gunned Down

The history of any prison seems to be highlighted by dramatic or violent escapes, and Oakalla certainly saw more than its fair share. The prison was almost conducive to escape: living conditions were harsh, and perimeter security was weak. Over nearly eight decades, more than 850 male and female prisoners made successful bids for freedom (see Appendix B).

August 11, 1926, was a scorching summer day. In the fields at the north end of the prison property, a group of about fifty prisoners were harvesting a field of hay under the heat of the afternoon sun. Deer Lake was a quarter mile to the east, and the inmates could hear the laughter of youngsters echoing across the water as they took relief from the heat. Although the work gangs were permitted to swim and bathe in the lake once a week during the summer, this group had to wait another three days before it would be their turn.

In the work gang were eighteen-year-old William Lane, and William Brewster, twenty-two. Lane had less than a year to serve on two burglary charges; Brewster had just been brought into Oakalla two weeks earlier, sentenced to twelve months for theft. Lane had never been imprisoned before, whereas Brewster had a fairly long record, and had been listed as an incorrigible by the juvenile authorities. Regardless, both men were liked by the guards and considered hard workers.

The group of prisoners were under the command of gang boss, Charles Boll, while security of the gang was maintained by Officers Edmond Coppin, Philip Cunningham, Larry Bulman, and George Rochfort. The men were well armed with side arms and repeating rifles.

As the gang neared the north end of the property, Officer Boll spotted Brewster and Lane leaning on their scythes, talking. The guard

Staff photo, circa 1920.

bellowed at the pair, reminding them there was no talking among prisoners and that they would spend the rest of the day in the "hole" if they didn't get back to work. The two men started chopping at the hay again, slightly in front of the rest of the group, as they continued north. A few minutes later they had worked their way so that they were now about thirty yards from the fence. Suddenly they dropped their tools and sprinted for the fence. Although they were wearing heavy work boots, the desperadoes raced across the field at lightning speed.

The guards yelled out, "Halt!" and "Stop or I'll shoot!," but their orders were ignored. The officers then crouched down, aiming low, and began firing a volley of shots at the escapees. With the sound of bullets singing around them, the two kept running until they were about to reach the fence. Just then there was a thud against Brewster's back. He let out a groan, stumbled, and fell to the ground. Lane continued on, but as he was about to start climbing the fence, he looked back at his pal writhing on the ground and knew it was over. He lifted his arms into the air and cried out, "Don't shoot!"

A total of twelve shots had been fired. One bullet penetrated Brewster's right hip and exited near his breast. The bullet's path had torn through several vital organs. While a guard took custody of Lane,

Inmates tending crops.

and another lowered his rifle at the rest of the group, to prevent further escape, Officer Boll ordered a third guard to run to the Main Gaol and fetch Dr. Murray.

The gaol surgeon was on scene within minutes, but there wasn't much he could do for the young man. Brewster had lost a lot of blood — the front of his prison garb was crimson. Attendants from Kingsway Ambulance Service were on scene a few minutes later and whisked the prisoner and an escorting guard away to Vancouver General Hospital, where Brewster was pronounced dead on arrival. This was the only incident in Oakalla's history where an inmate was shot to death by a guard.

Bailey and Yaoki Executed

The third consecutive double hanging at Oakalla Prison was that of Kenneth Roosevelt Bailey, a cat burglar who shot and killed a home-owner during a robbery attempt that went awry, and Nichi Yaoki, a marine-fireman who went berserk during an argument and hacked a Mrs. Takahashi to death with an axe. The public hanging of these two exemplified striking contrasts in emotions that doomed prisoners have displayed as they met the hangman's noose.

Before his execution, Yaoki received spiritual counselling and was remorseful for his crime. Bailey, on the other hand, refused all religious help and showed no signs of grief or apprehension. In the chilly morning hours of January 9, 1925, when the condemned men were brought out of their cells and into the open courtyard, Yaoki appeared faint and needed to be supported by guards as he approached the gallows. Bailey, on the other hand, made an impressive last show of bravado. As he approached the gallows, he walked proudly, head held high, as if he were the honoured guest at a reception. Then as Ellis, the executioner, swiftly went about his work binding the legs of the men and placing hoods over their heads, Bailey began to act as if he were directing him in his work. "Give us service!" he shouted from beneath the mask. Moments later he commanded, "Let 'er go!" As a white mist of hot breath escaped through Bailey's mask, Ellis obliged and released the trap door.[7]

By the end of the Roaring Twenties, lavishness and free-spirited prosperity prevailed in cities throughout North America, and Vancouver was certainly no exception. However, within the walls of Oakalla, only a few miles away in the tranquil suburb of Burnaby, conditions were still austere. The wardens maintained a tight rein of control over their prisoners which would continue for at least another fifteen years. While there were few major incidents during these early years, the 1920s brought an end to Oakalla's innocence as a quiet rural gaol. The blood of prisoners had been spilled and ten men had been sent to their deaths. It was just the beginning.

Three

Maintaining Discipline
1929-1943

On June 1, 1929, William McMynn retired and was succeeded as Oakalla's new warden by Inspector Walter Owen, former assistant to the superintendent of the B.C. Provincial Police. Owen's distinguished career began in 1899 when he joined the force in Atlin. Three years later he was the city's chief constable. In 1914 he moved to Vancouver to become an assistant inspector, where he remained until 1923 when he transferred to Victoria and was appointed as an inspector.

For Walter Owen, world events quickly affected his smooth operation of the prison. In October 1929 the stock market crashed, sending industrialized nations into deep depression. In British Columbia, thousands of workers were laid off with virtually no social assistance. Hundreds of vagrants wandered the streets of Vancouver, many of them resorting to minor property crimes. In no time, a steady stream wound up behind bars at Oakalla. This became a source of conflict between Warden Owen and Vancouver Chief Constable Bingham. Owen complained to the Attorney-General's Department that within a six-month period more than three hundred prisoners sentenced to five days or less had been brought to Oakalla from the city lockup. Many of them were filthy and covered with vermin. The vagrants had infested Oakalla with scabies, lice, and fleas. Bingham argued that there were no facilities to house the prisoners or ensure their cleanliness at the police station. When the Warden threatened to refuse the prisoners, Bingham retorted that his men would then simply drop them off at the front gate. In the end, Owen had no choice but to continue taking them in, and try to ensure that each man was thoroughly bathed before entering the cellblocks.

His initial attempt at controlling infestation was unsuccessful. The first in a series of complaints over conditions within Oakalla was brought forward in the Provincial Legislature in March 1930. In response to these reports Attorney-General Pooley toured the prison to investigate first hand. To his dismay he found it quite dirty and a "strange contrast" to the Dominion Penitentiary in New Westminster. A month later he was confronted by allegations of smuggling, drug traffic, wine making, and the mixing of young offenders and habitual criminals in Oakalla. "I have no report of such conditions as alleged," he stated, "and as far as I know there is absolutely no truth in the story."[1] In May a Grand Jury inspected the facility and was also critical of the insufficient number of guards, overcrowding, idle prisoners, unclean cells, and a need for improved sanitary arrangements. Owen was disturbed by all the controversy and he immediately began to oversee some changes.

When the Attorney-General had toured the prison in the previous year, he had been shocked by the high number of prisoners he found "lolling about" during working hours. In response, Owen set up a sheet metal shop, which began production of all provincial automobile license plates. Over the next few years, prison industries included manufacturing clothing, boots, and straw-filled mattresses. By the mid-1930s the Warden was also able to rid Oakalla of much of the insect infestation that had earlier caused him grief. However, he had no way of dealing with the ever present rise in the inmate population which had now surpassed a daily rate of more than 400. For Owen, and the wardens to follow, it was a source of constant frustration.

The Escape of Wilcox and McDougall
On the evening of December 19, 1930, Vancouver Police Constable Daugherty responded to a prowler complaint in the area of Main and Alexander streets. He found a man in the vicinity matching the description and started to question him. While the officer was talking to the suspect, two men emerged from the shadows, and

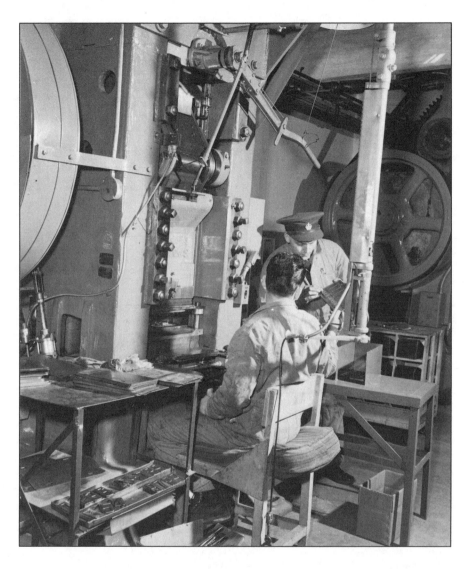

Oakalla produced automobile license plates from 1930-1975.

severely beat him. Fortunately the officer was able to get a good look at the men before they fled. One was about twenty, tall and slim, and had a scar on his forehead that cut through his right eyebrow. The officer thought he recognized the crook and, after searching through a collection of police mug shots, he picked him out. The man was Ellis Wilcox, a local who had a record for violence and robbery.

Four days later, at about nine p.m., Wilcox and three other men burst into a general store in Fraser Mills, owned by Mr. Lim Sing.

Three brandished revolvers and a fourth man, about five-foot-two, waved a sawed-off shotgun. "Stick 'em up!" he yelled. Before being pushed to the floor, Sing looked at the bandit. The sallow-faced little man was in his mid-twenties, had a pencil-thin moustache, and a constant smirk on his face. Fraser McDougall, the "grinning bandit," had struck again. Several Chinese customers were herded into a back room and relieved of their wallets and watches, while two of the gunmen went behind the front counter and raided the till. The proprietor had just made a large withdrawal from the bank so he could cash the mill-workers' pay cheques, allowing the crooks to net over $2,000. The four men then backed out of the store, climbed into an awaiting car, and drove off towards Pitt River Road.

Over the Christmas holiday season, the Lower Mainland broke out in a rash of banditry, but local police forces had a good idea who were committing the crimes. On December 31, ten men were arrested at various locations on robbery charges. Four, including Wilcox, were charged with the Chinese store holdup. Wilcox was also charged with the assault on Constable Daugherty. The following day, McDougall was picked up at his home at 1809 Vanness Avenue by Detectives Munroe and Bell. On January 8, they appeared before the Magistrate at Maillardville and were committed for trial on the Fraser Mills robbery. A week later, Wilcox and McDougall were also charged with three other holdups in the Vancouver area and lodged in Oakalla to await the assizes.

It wasn't the first time this pair had been in Oakalla, and they still had a number of acquaintances on the inside who were able to help keep them in contact with friends on the outside. The two felons knew that, if convicted, they would probably be looking at a minimum of twenty years. The high cement walls surrounding the heavily guarded New Westminster Penitentiary made escape almost impossible. If they wanted to make a break, it would have to be from Oakalla.

It was about 6:40 p.m. on March 5, 1931, and darkness had just fallen. In the rear lane of the Vancouver Court House an unoccupied Provincial Police paddy wagon was parked, waiting to take the day's last prisoners back to Oakalla. A young man in a dark cap and long coat on the nearby street corner looked around nervously. He waited for some people to pass, then approached the rear of the police vehicle. He swung open the unlocked door, and from under his coat he pulled out a bulky cloth sack which he slid under the prisoner's wooden bench. Closing the door, he hurriedly left the area.

It had been a long day for the two crooks; Wilcox had been acquitted of one robbery and McDougall convicted of another. However, both were still awaiting trial on other charges. Shortly before seven, the two were pat-frisked by Provincial Police Constable Robert Simms, who in the company of Constable Ben Greenhough, handcuffed them and escorted the men from the building and into the rear of the wagon. After a half hour journey out to Burnaby, the wagon pulled up to the front steps of the Main Gaol. The policemen were met at the top of the stairs by Officer Brown who opened the barred door for them. The prisoners were brought to the front counter and had their handcuffs removed. Brown took one of his two sets of keys and opened the door to let the officers out. He bid them farewell and locked it behind him.

Wilcox and McDougall sat on a bench in the front hall, while Thomas Rutledge, a young rookie, stood behind the counter and filled out the paperwork. After a few minutes, the officer said that Wilcox was booked in and could return to the West Wing. The prisoner stood, adjusted the pants of his baggy suit, and followed Brown as he went to open the door to Centre Hall. As Brown grabbed his keys, a blunt object jabbed him in the middle of his back. Wilcox showed the guard his pistol and said, "Let's go back to the front counter."

At about the same time Officer Rutledge had left the counter to put some documents away. While his back was turned McDougall drew two revolvers from his waist-band. "Hey kid!," he called out. Rutledge spun around to find the little man pointing both guns at him. The convict came around the counter and told the guard to lie on the floor. Wilcox and his hostage then returned to the room and Brown was told to lie beside Rutledge. For the moment the prisoners and the two guards were the only people in the Administration Wing. The prisoners dashed to the front door — only to find it was locked from the inside. When the prisoners left the two guards, Brown had placed the front door keys on a shelf behind the counter. Seconds later Wilcox returned to the men on the floor. He stooped over Officer Brown and placed the barrel of the gun to the back of his head. "Give me your keys or I'll blow your damned brains out." In a dangerous attempt to frustrate the escape, Brown handed over the wrong set of keys. The prisoner tried the front door and when he realized what had happened, he went wild. He started kicking the guard and threatened to shoot him. The two officers covered their heads and refused to speak. The felons panicked, wanting to find the keys before anyone discovered what was happening. They were afraid of ending up in a shoot-out, trapped inside the prison. Desperately they searched the area, and Wilcox eventually found the keys on his own.

At that time Victoria City Police Constable Walter Andrews, his prisoner, and a taxi-cab driver, who had just come to pick up a discharged man, entered Oakalla grounds and walked up the stairs to the front gate. To their surprise they were met with three handguns pointing at their heads. They were brought inside the building and told to join the two guards behind the counter. The bandits relieved Andrews of his revolver and asked the Victoria prisoner if he wanted to join them in their escape. He wisely refused. The pair then took the taxi-driver hostage, had him drive them off grounds and into the city, where they released him.

In the days that followed, the fugitives managed to elude capture, although they had been spotted in a New Westminster Chinese restaurant, and were identified as the pair who stole a truck belonging to Rev. Fallis. On March 11, a truck driver and a young man spotted two tramps camped out in the bush near Imperial Street and 29th Avenue in Burnaby, and reported it to the police. Constable Holliday of the British Columbia Police investigated the sighting, taking the two men along with him to point out the area. When they got to the site the armed escapees heard them coming and had the drop on them. Mc-Dougall hid in the bush, but Wilcox remained in plain view. At first the officer didn't recognize Wilcox and was going to simply tell him to move along. Then McDougall came up from behind, with his gun held out towards the constable. He told Holliday to raise his hands and took his service revolver. The pair then robbed the two accompanying men, ran over to where they had ditched their stolen truck, and drove off.

Two days later, Burnaby Police were once again tipped-off to a sighting of the escapees hanging around a sedan parked near Boundary Road and Grandview Highway. This time Chief Constable Devitt took no chances. He loaded his car with a Ross rifle and shotgun and had Constable Noel Pennington accompany him. He also had two motor-cycle officers guard the nearby highways in case they escaped. The two men spotted the suspect vehicle parked on 19th Street between Boundary Road and Smith Avenue. They parked on Smith Avenue, about a block away from the suspects, and decided to approach on foot. Chief Devitt, a champion marksman, grabbed the rifle and started walking through the bushes towards the car. Pennington took the shotgun, walked south on Smith Avenue and then started coming down 19th Street. Chief Devitt related the following encounter:

> When I was about 20 yards from the car, I called out
> to them to surrender — that we were police officers.
> Wilcox was standing, then, just at the back of the car,

which had been driven off the road at right angles into the bush. He did not seem to be armed; but suddenly he pulled out two revolvers and started to fire. I heard the bullets singing over my head; but, in the excitement, I could not say how many shots he fired.

And then I let him have it. My shot struck his trigger finger, smashing it. It seemed to me that he pulled the dangling finger off, and tossed it into the bush. Then he staggered backwards and collapsed.

McDougall had run around the front of the car and was banging away. I fired at him once. I don't know if the bullet went through the windshield or not; but there was a mark near one of McDougall's eyes, after he had surrendered, that looked as though he had been sprayed with flying glass.

Constable Pennington was coming down 19th Street, with a shotgun, and McDougall, seeing him, realized that he was trapped in the open. I guess he didn't like the look of that shot-gun much either.

I shouted to him to put them up; and then a moment later I again told him to put them up or I would drill him. McDougall then put up his hands, and Pennington coming down the road, disarmed him and we put the cuffs on him.

Then we did the best that we could for Wilcox.[2]

Wilcox died almost instantly; the rifle shot that severed his finger had ricochetted off one of his revolvers and into his abdomen. McDougall was taken into custody and returned to Oakalla. He was eventually transferred to the B.C. Penitentiary where he served a lengthy sentence for a wide variety of offences.

Hangings Moved Indoors
The last execution in the courtyard of the Old Gaol was that of Bill Mathoff on September 4, 1931. Later that year, a small, low-ceilinged room, on the second floor of the South Wing was converted into the new gallows. Witnesses, the press, and other officials were ushered into the execution chamber and directed to stand behind a barrier at one end. On the floor in the middle of the room were two four-by-three-foot wooden doors that were three-quarters encircled by a metal railing. Beside them was a lever that would release a latch and allow the trap doors to fall open. Above the doors was a

Boarded Gallows; trap-door lever on right.

sturdy iron beam, to which the executioner would attach one end of the rope. At the bottom of the shaft, in the basement of the prison, was where the prison physician waited for the plummeting body.

The Bagley Gang

A decade of Prohibition and the growing drug trade had brought wealth and establishment to Vancouver's criminal underworld. By the 1930s there was a marked rise in organized crime on the West Coast, with an emergence of smaller and more violent gangs vying for a piece of the action. Undoubtedly, the most notorious gangster Oakalla had to contend with during this era was William Bagley. The ruthlessness of this balding, quiet-mannered man first became apparent in 1926 while he was serving an eight-year sentence at the British Columbia Penitentiary for the armed robbery of a Nanaimo hotel. It was discovered that he had masterminded a shocking plan in which several inmates would rush the guards while the rest of the prisoners were on sick parade with the doctor. They would disarm them, raid the armouries, kill the guards in the tower, and make their escape. Luckily, this plan was thwarted before it ever materialized.

Bagley went straight to work again when he was released from the Penitentiary in the spring of 1931. After only two months of freedom, a warrant was issued for his arrest in connection with a safe-cracking at the Harrison Hot Springs Hotel. The thirty-nine-year-old's distinguishable features like his big nose, glasses, and stooped shoulders made him easily recognizable and it wasn't long before he was picked up by Washington State Police and remanded in the Bellingham Gaol to await his extradition hearing. Here he made another escape attempt when he managed to have a gun secreted into the gaol. He pulled his sidearm on the guard in the holding tank and attempted to shoot his way out. The officer's life was spared when Bagley's gun misfired three times. The gaoler returned fire with his own weapon, shooting at Bagley four times; one bullet hit him in the leg. Bagley surrendered and was taken to hospital. Several months later the extradition went ahead and he was transferred to Oakalla. Convicted of the safe-cracking charge, Bagley was sentenced to fourteen years and fifteen lashes.

During his appeal period, he caused all kinds of problems for Walter Owen and his staff. In September 1931 he attempted to have an automatic .32 calibre pistol, three files, three hacksaws, and a bottle of ammonia smuggled into the prison. Members of his gang living in the community had placed them in a hollowed-out log near the fence line. Contacts within the prison were to pick up the items when they were doing grounds maintenance. The plan was foiled when the contraband was found by a guard's fourteen-year-old son who went fishing at a creek near the prison property. Several weeks later, officials received word that four hacksaw blades would be smuggled in. Guards closely searched all incoming material and found two blades taped inside a magazine. The other two blades would not be found for another month.

Around Christmas, 1931, Bagley was transferred from the South Wing to the third tier of the West Wing, where he joined eighteen other inmates. On the tier were William Lane, 23, who in 1926 had attempted to escape with inmate Brewster but gave up upon seeing his buddy gunned down; Gordon Fawcett, 21, a muscular young man who was captured in October when he and two other men attempted to rob the Bank of Montreal at Sixteenth and Cambie. Fawcett was wounded when the teller grabbed a revolver and shot him; Frank Sorge, 24, who was appealing a four-year conviction for possessing burglary tools; and Norman Moore, 25, who had just been sentenced to eighteen months for breaking and entering Pitman's Store in Burnaby's Central Park.

Moore was a small-time crook and didn't really know any of the other men on his tier. He told other people that he was an electrician but that times were tough and he did the break-in because he was penniless and couldn't get work. However his record indicated a long history of petty property offences and that he had just been released from the penitentiary for the same thing. At about two o'clock Sunday afternoon on January 3, 1932, Moore was sitting reading outside his cell at the far end of the corridor when he noticed a faint crack in the v-joint of the bars that covered the tier window. When he went over to the bars and began to pick at the crack with his finger nail, Moore was surprised at how easily the "metal" began to crumble away. Picking up a piece, he realized that it was soap that had been discoloured and packed into the grooves.

"Get away from there!" Frank Sorge yelled, coming up behind him.

"What's the game?" said Moore, raising an eyebrow.

"None of your damn business," Sorge said. Sorge then took off down the tier and returned a few minutes later with William Bagley. They took Moore into his cell and Bagley pushed him onto the bed saying, "You tell anyone about this and I'll slit your throat."

"I swear to God I won't say a word," Moore pleaded, "I want to go with you, I want to break out too."

Bagley and Sorge discussed this and decided it was better to allow Moore to come with them than risk him squealing to the guards. Bagley told Moore that it was all going to go down after supper lock-up.

By 4:30 p.m. the inmates had been served their meals and the prison was locked down to allow staff to have their breaks. The only inmates who remained out of their cells were the "trusties" who would pick up the meal-trays from in front of the cells and mop the tier. At about 6:00 p.m., Bagley and the others appeared in front of Moore's cell. "Let's go, kid," whispered the leader. Bagley took out a foot-long flat bar and slid it up between the cell gate and the frame, into the locking pins. Slowly he lifted the latches and they quietly rolled the door open. No one trusted the tier-cleaner and Moore asked where he was. One of the men told him not to worry as they had locked him in his cell so he couldn't go downstairs and tell the guards. They then went to the far end of the tier, and easily removed the pre-cut bars. The four young men felt they could hang from the ledge and safely drop to the ground from that height, but Bagley said his leg was still weak from the Bellingham Gaol shooting and tied several sheets to the frame so that he could lower himself. The leader went first and the rest followed, Moore being the last. Under the cover of darkness they dropped twenty feet to the ground and started to run towards Royal Oak Avenue. Moore saw Bagley, Fawcett, and Sorge run towards the southwest corner of the property, heading towards Kingsway, and knew that they wouldn't want him around. He saw Lane heading north, down the hill towards Royal Oak Avenue, and decided to join up with him. He caught up to the escapee as he started to climb the fence. Lane looked back at Moore and said, "You idiot. You scared the hell out of me, I thought you were a guard." The pair laughed as they scaled the fence and disappeared down the street.

The escape was not noticed until a staff member made his rounds at 7:00 p.m. The local police forces were notified and an intensive search was mounted. Shortly after noon the following day Vancouver Police Sergeant Charles Thomas and Constable Slattery were walking south on Prince Edward Street near Mountain View Cemetery, after being informed of suspicious persons seen in the area. The men started walking into the wooded area when they saw something moving. The officers called for reinforcements, and they began to comb the bush with their guns drawn. A few minutes later they found Lane hiding face down beneath a stump. His face scratched and prison clothing torn, the escapee was taken into custody without a struggle. The sergeant grabbed him by the scruff of the neck, "Where's your pals kid? Are they with you?" Lane wouldn't say a word. More officers were summoned to the area and within minutes Norman Moore was found nearby. There were other possible sightings of Bagley and Fawcett later that day at the Kitsilano Indian Reserve and the UBC Endowment Lands, but the search failed to turn up the fugitives. Police armed with sub-machine guns were also stationed at major bridges and highways and checked all motorists without success.

After the break-out was made public, two guards were immediately suspended, and an investigation into the security of the prison was ordered by the Attorney General. Several days later, Attorney General Pooley stated that a wall would be built around the institution, like the one at the B.C. Penitentiary, and Oakalla's fences would be electrified with 500 volts of electricity flowing through them.[3] A wall was never built and, from what can be determined, the fence was never electrified.

The police had staked out all the known hang-outs and homes of the fugitives. January 7, this paid off, when Sorge returned to his mother's house at 3908 Slocan Street to get a change of clothes and a glass of milk. At about eight a.m. that day Mrs. Sorge had just returned home, after dropping her daughter off at work, when there was a knock at the back door. Her fugitive son came in soaked from head to toe, his face worn and pale. "Oh, Frank, Frank, why don't you give yourself up?" she cried. "They'll catch you and shoot you.

I know you'll get shot."

"Don't take it so hard, mother," he said. "Don't worry about me, I just want to get some clothes." The escapee then went out to the front porch to get the morning milk. As he bent down to pick up the glass bottles he looked down the street and saw a man in a suit standing at the corner. "The detectives have been watching the house since you escaped," his mother said. "Oh Frank, please stay and give yourself up."[4]

Sorge went back inside and poured a glass a milk. After gulping it down he shook his head and said, "I'm going, mother." The fugitive then ran out the back door and down a lane.

Detectives Branca and Morrison had been watching the Slocan house. When they realized that Sorge had returned there and left they started to search the Grandview Highway area. Mr. Doman, a service station owner, spotted the escapee while driving along Victoria Drive; recognizing him from a picture in the *Vancouver Sun*. He found the two detectives walking along Grandview Highway and drove them to where he had last seen the escapee. When they returned to the area, Sorge was still walking along the side of the road. The policemen jumped from the car and one lowered a sawed-off shotgun at him while the other handcuffed and searched the prisoner. Sorge had concealed a loaded .32-calibre revolver and fifteen extra rounds. Fortunately for the apprehending officers, the gun had slipped down Sorge's waistband and stuck in his pant-leg.

Bagley and Fawcett continued to elude the police for months. The newspapers speculated as to their whereabouts; most notable was the belief that Bagley was in Seattle with an old lover. As with all escapes, the police were deluged with sightings of the pair; all turned out to be fruitless.

However, on March 26, 1932, Game Warden "Slim" Cameron came across the pair driving along a back road in the Ladner area. He recognized Bagley, and single-handedly attempted to arrest the escapees. He proved to be no match for the crooks who were always armed. They took his gun, stole his wallet, handcuffed him in the rear of his vehicle and drove into Burnaby, where they tied Cameron to a tree. The pair decided to split up as they left the game warden. Fawcett drove the stolen truck into downtown Vancouver to buy some ammunition. But city detectives had been tipped-off to his location and arrested him behind the Terminal Hotel.

A few hours later, Bagley walked into Harry Royle's confectionery store on Hastings Street in Burnaby. He robbed the store at gunpoint and commandeered customer Ronald Chasney and his car. Royle called the police, and forty-seven-year-old Burnaby Detective Dave Maxwell was on scene within minutes. The owner told him he last saw Bagley and the hostage-driver heading west towards Vancouver. Maxwell raced along Hastings and caught up to the car at Clark Drive. He motioned to the driver to pull over to the curb. When Chasney stopped the car, Bagley jumped out the passenger side and fired at Maxwell four times with his .45 calibre pistol. Three of the bullets found their target; striking him in the arm, stomach, and liver. The officer dropped to the ground, critically wounded. Bagley then forced Chasney out of his car, and used it to make a get-away. As Maxwell lay in serious condition at Vancouver General Hospital, local police forces and the community were outraged over the dastardly crime. The officer was very popular with the city's youths and had an excellent service record. But Maxwell had a strong will to live, and he eventually recovered and was released from hospital.

Bagley was able to flee to the United States, where he continued to lead a life of crime, until he was eventually arrested and sent to prison. Once again he made a violent escape attempt, and this time, the gaol-break cost a prison guard his life. On September 6, 1935, William Bagley was hanged in San Quentin Penitentiary; bringing to an end the violent life of the Pacific Northwest's most notorious gangster. Although Oakalla would not have to deal with such a desperate man for a number of years, the prison was not yet free of the troubles caused by his partner, Gordon Fawcett.

Escape Through the Gallows
After being returned to Oakalla, and serving a number of years in gaol, Fawcett was released and continued practicing his trade of armed hold-ups. In December 1936, Fawcett was arrested on a warrant issued by Port Moody and Coquitlam Police relating to various alleged offences, including theft of auto, unlawfully possessing a weapon, and attempted murder. Once again he was waiting trial in Oakalla when he decided to make another bid for freedom. The career criminal recruited boyish-looking Vernon "Blackie" Campbell to assist him in the plot. The two also had the assistance of at least one other insider, and although it was never proven, many believed that a staff member was involved in the escape.

At that time the South Wing handled all potentially high-risk remand inmates, who were also allowed special privileges over the rest of the prison population; they were permitted to wear their own civilian clothing and were not locked in their individual cells during meal periods. This was because they were still waiting trial or had not yet been sentenced by the courts. After several weeks of careful planning, two men took advantage of these regulations.

At 4:30 p.m., on April 4, 1937, the prison was locked down for meal periods, and these prisoners were only restricted to the corridors of each tier. Both inmates were lodged on the right side of the third tier; Campbell in the first cell and Fawcett in the last. They placed crude dummies under the sheets of their beds and walked up to the end gate of the corridor. According to the prison report, the gate had a loose screw, and the lock could be opened from the inside. The men opened the gate and made their way down a flight of stairs to the landing of the second tier. On this level was a set of doors leading to the execution chamber.

How they managed to enter the gallows remains a mystery. At the entrance was a barred locking metal gate, and just behind it a solid wooden door that could only be locked from the outside. Somehow the convicts were able to pick the locks to both doors (either by key or replica), and enter the room. The interesting factor is that the door was then locked behind them, by either another inmate or guard, and the pair were able to work in privacy at a barred window inside the room. Using a smuggled hacksaw blade or file, the pair sawed through the bars within an hour. The gallows were also used as a store-room so there were plenty of sheets and blankets around to make a rope with. They tied the rope to the window and lowered themselves to the ground where they made a mad dash for the south fence, which was especially risky as it was still daylight.

Five years earlier, a portion of Oakalla had been loaned to the British Columbia Provincial Police who formed a ten-man mounted squad, and a section of the Old Gaol was used as barracks for the men stationed there. During the escape two officers had been upstairs looking out a window when they spotted the fugitives scale the fence. They ran outside and down the road, raising the hue and cry, but the escapees, dressed in everyday attire, had not aroused the attention of any passerby. Someone later reported that they had seen the two men get into a waiting vehicle on nearby Selma Avenue. While police scoured the Lower Mainland, the provincial government placed a $250 reward on the head of each man. Several days later, the intensive search for the desperadoes was called off when the suspect vehicle, stolen from a local lumber company, was recovered in Bellingham. The two men were never seen together again.

Several months later, on May 27, Campbell attempted an armed hold-up in Tacoma, but the robbery was botched and he was shot to death outside the bank by the local police. Fawcett did not turn up until 1941, when he was arrested in California and sentenced to 18 months. When he completed his gaol term he was transferred to Oakalla and later sent to the Penitentiary.

First Prisoners' Revolt

By the mid-1930s the increasing number of security-risk inmates in Oakalla began to take a toll on maintaining an orderly institution. Some were beginning to rebel against the strict discipline imposed by the Warden. The first recorded disturbance began on Good Friday, April 10, 1936. The uprising started when a group of nearly forty men refused to eat their roast beef dinner. The food strike extended into a work stoppage and was supported by most of the inmate population. This carried on throughout the holiday weekend, and reporters who had assembled outside the prison, could occasionally hear the shouts of inmates. Although the disturbance had been minor, the Warden felt that he was loosing control. Owen and other prison administrators petitioned the government to increase the severity and types of punishments so that Oakalla could maintain the discipline observed in earlier years. In 1936 the Provincial Gaol Rules and Regulations were amended to allow for further disciplinary action against insubordinates:

> (c) shackle prisoner to cell-gate during working-hours;
>
> (d) flogging with the leather paddle or strap upon receipt of a certificate from the Prison Surgeon that the prisoner is physically fit to undergo corporal punishment;
>
> (f) confinement in cell without bed or lights."[5]

Use of a paddle and flogging inmates with a whip had been used at Oakalla before 1936, however, it could only be employed when ordered by the courts as part of a sentence. The paddle was a three-foot stiff-leather strap with holes perforating its broad surface. The holes decreased wind resistance, while also creating a suctioning effect when used. A prisoners backside would be covered with tender and bleeding welts caused by these holes. The whip, or cat-o'-nine-tails, was reserved for more heinous crimes such as rape, armed burglary, robbery, and indecent assault. The Regulations excluded females prisoners from corporal punishment. When guards were authorized to whip or paddle an offender, he would be strapped by his arms and legs to a table, his trousers lowered, and a black hood placed over his head. The warden would hand one of the guards the paddle or whip, and then the officers would shuffle around the table. This would ensure

43

that the recipient would never know exactly who meted out the punishment.

Punishment was also administered by placing unruly prisoners in isolation or segregation cells. The original Dark Cells were in the dirt-floored basement beneath the Administration Wing of the Old Gaol. The boiler room and steam pipes were near the punishment cellar which created almost unbearable heat. Prison Doctor Guy Richmond wrote that it was amazing that no life was ever lost in these cells, and "inmates had to rely on infrequent visits of a prison officer, and their only companions were the rats."[6] By 1940, Warden Owen had already made several pleas to the government to fund the construction of new punishment facilities.

A Triple Hanging

The only triple execution at Oakalla, and just the second in British Columbia's judicial history, was carried out on November 6, 1936, when Eneas George, his brother Richardson George, and Charles Russell were simultaneously hanged. Controversy surrounded this execution when, ten years after the incident, a local newspaper reported that one of the prisoners was in fact a woman — "Inez George" — but offered no proof to substantiate the claim.[7] Nonetheless, from this date forward many staff members and officials at the prison have also claimed that a female offender was once hanged. In July 1991, the *Vancouver Sun* continued to fuel the rumour in a summary of the prison's history.[8] It's ironic that a reporter from the same newspaper attended the triple hanging in 1936 and described Eneas George as a Native Indian male, the younger brother of Richardson George.

The Indians were two of three brothers who had been convicted of slaying Indian Police Constable Francis Gisborne on May 23, 1934. The third brother received a life sentence for the crime.

Charles Russell was one of four men involved in a Vancouver bank robbery in January 1936, in which a bank teller had been shot to death. Two of the men involved in the robbery committed suicide with their own weapons when police attempted to apprehend them. The fourth man, Earl Dunbar, the driver of the "get-away" car, was executed at Oakalla 21 days later.

Owen Opens Oakalla to Press

Criticism of conditions within the prison continued to make their way to Victoria during the 1930s. Released inmates, and visiting friends or family members, all related a variety of stories which

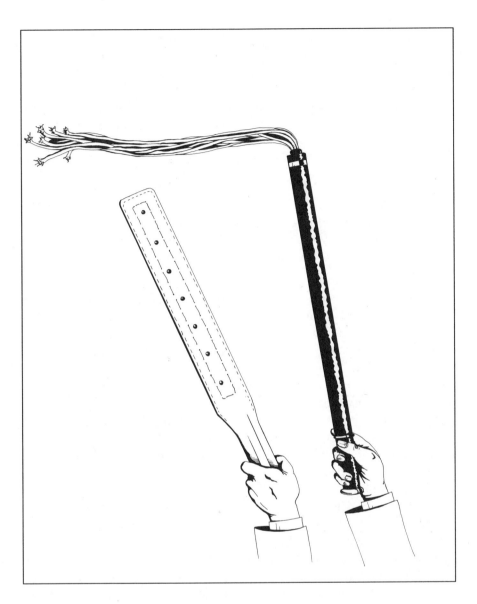

Instruments of punishment: Lash and Paddle.

appeared to indicate that once again all was not well within the prison. Warden Owen strongly disagreed. In a move that would be repeated many times, he attempted to dispel allegations of cruel living conditions by allowing a member of the press to tour the prison. In late 1937 Province reporter Norm Hacking toured the centre and documented his findings:

> Oakalla is not a brutal, cold, inhuman institution. On

the contrary, the majority of the prison employees have the welfare of the inmates at heart within their limitations, and actual prison life has many redeeming qualities.

As a prison establishment Oakalla is scrupulously clean, it is modern in its layout and equipment, and is practically self-sufficient. It is run more economically than any other gaol of its kind in Canada.[9]

Hacking's only criticism was that Oakalla was poorly segregated and gave opportunity for "impressionable young men to learn the mysteries of law evasion and organized crime." The Warden's strategy worked: following this report, almost a full decade passed before conditions at Oakalla were once again criticized.

New Gaol for Women

As far back as 1930, it had been announced that a separate prison for women would soon be constructed. But the Depression left the government in a state where it could only make promises at best. The projected costs of building a new facility were too high, especially considering that in 1933 Vancouver's schools were about to close for lack of funds. During this time, the women's quarters moved from the South Wing of the Main Gaol to the officially condemned Old Gaol's West Wing. It was a more favourable setting for the women because its exercise yard was much larger than the cordoned-off section of the roof of the Main Gaol, and inmates were housed in dormitories of six to eight prisoners instead of in individual cells.

Good news finally came in January 1939, when $50,000 was allocated for the construction of the prison. The building would be two stories high and capable of housing forty-two prisoners. Construction was completed in November 1940, with the final cost being $14,000 over budget. On November 16, Attorney-General Gordon Wismer conducted the opening ceremonies before a host of local politicians, media, and members of community support groups who had rallied for many years to see this day. Three days after the fanfare, the first gaol in British Columbia built exclusively for female offenders opened its gates, and immediately filled, with forty new inmates.

Owen Retires

Back in the Men's Unit, each passing year was accompanied by another series of hangings. Few of the trials and executions were as sensational as "Cannonball" Baker's, most were the final chapter

Oakalla Women's Correctional Centre.

in a senseless story of despair which ended in murder. The execution of Frank Sylvester was one such story. The Native Indian was hanged on January 24, 1941, for the murders of two elderly white men in Windermere Valley in October 1940. The twenty-one-year-old alcoholic desperately wanted to get his hands on a drink, so he rode his horse through the valley until he came upon Ernie Foster's secluded mansion. Bringing with him a high powered rifle, Sylvester murdered Foster and a friend in cold blood. He stole a small quantity of liquor and then torched the house in an attempt to conceal the murders. He went to get back on his horse, but the rifle's blast had spooked the beast, and it had fled. Sylvester then stole the owner's car, which eventually tied him to the murders. On the day he was to be executed, he was asked if he had any last request. "Take care of my horse," was the young man's response. "My horse was the last friend I had." At the murder trial, Sylvester's own brother and cousin testified against him.[10]

A serious escape also marred the final years of Owen's long service record. At about three p.m. on May 29, 1942, an inmate working in the license plate shop complained that his shoes were falling apart. A guard was called to escort him to the shoe shop. When he and the guard arrived, the prisoner met with three accomplices who were pretending to repair worn out footwear. As the escorting officer entered the shop, he and the guard in the workshop were attacked by the four inmates; one of whom used a hammer as a weapon during the struggle. The escapees then ran out of the building and scaled the property fence. By this time other staff members had been informed of the escape attempt and were closing in on the fugitives. Within several hours all four were back behind Oakalla's bars.

During his fourteen-year tenure, Walter Owen had witnessed the beginning of disruptions, protests, and other forms of rebellion. Escapes were also becoming more violent and daring. These disturbing trends were to continue in the tenure of his successor.

Four

Rebellion Ferments
1943-1952

When Walter Owen retired in July 1943, he was replaced by Deputy Warden John Millman. It was a smooth transition, and Millman coasted through his first year. Shortly thereafter, however, things began to heat up.

In what was believed to be an act of spontaneous combustion, the prison's winter hay supply caught fire on August 2, 1944. The burning hay set the cattle barn ablaze, and the fire quickly spread from the wooden structure to the farm equipment sheds. As tongues of fire shot up into the night sky, the Burnaby Fire Department and a group of prisoners called the "Oakalla Prison Farm Volunteer Fire Brigade," were called into action. Despite the intense heat, they managed to save six horses and most of the farm machinery. Unfortunately, along with 80 tons of hay, the barn was completely destroyed.

That December, the Warden was called before a Coroner's Inquest which was investigating the death of Sidney Ellis, a forty-four-year-old inmate serving a twenty-month sentence for possession of narcotics and house breaking instruments. The jury concluded that Ellis had died of accidental poisoning, from lead that was contained in opium. Evidence indicated that an opium solution had been absorbed and then dried in a handkerchief. The handkerchief, however, contained particles of lead. Ellis had strained the opium out from the cloth and was poisoned when he drank the mixture. It was one of the first reports of drug smuggling in Oakalla.

Just over a year later, the Warden triumphantly announced that Oakalla staff had stopped dope smuggling by refusing to allow visitors to bring tobacco products in for the inmates. Apparently the drugs were mixed in with pouches of tobacco. From then on, inmates could only purchase these products through the canteen. This restriction curtailed the flow of drugs into Oakalla only briefly, despite the Warden's optimism. Prisoners soon found ingenious new ways of bringing drugs and other contraband into the gaol. "Suitcasing" contraband became the most common method of smuggling, which still exists today.[1]

Executioner's Fatal Error

From the first hanging at Oakalla in 1919 to the mid-1940s there had been three successive official hangmen in Canada. The men led secretive lives; all assumed aliases, and they rarely made public statements. The first hangman, who used the name Arthur Ellis, was the longest serving executioner; he served more than twenty years before retiring in 1939. By most accounts he was incredibly adept at his job and worked with "lightning speed." He must have had some military background as he always saluted prison officials during the formalities leading up to an execution. However, on one occasion (the execution of Dominico Nassa, in 1929) the hanging had to be delayed for nearly two hours as he had not yet arrived at the prison. One newspaper claimed that he had been found in the drunk tank at the Burnaby Police Station shortly before the hanging.[2] After his retirement,"Sam Edwards" replaced him, but presided over only one hanging at Oakalla: the execution of an elderly black man, R. A. Wright on June 16, 1939. By the hanging of Frank Sylvester in 1941, "John Ellis" had taken over the role as Canada's official executioner.

Ellis was described as a "dapper" little man, who was usually quiet and sombre. "A sharp contrast from the free-and-easy manner of the late 'Arthur Ellis'."[3] While making his way to one particular hanging he was approached by two reporters for an interview. "It's a grim job," he replied to their questions, "the less said about it the better." When asked how he got into the field of hangings he stated: "It's an easy business to get into — but hard to get out of."[4]

Up until the hanging of Byron Bruce Potter on January 10, 1946, these hangmen had carried out each hanging without error. Although it was rare that the condemned man's neck would be broken, thus ensuring instantaneous death (most died from suffocation), all hangings proceeded basically as planned. On this date, that all changed. As in previous hangings, prior to the execution Ellis would use sand bags equal to the weight of the prisoner to test the rope and noose to ensure that the rope was tied off at a specific length so that the body would drop a sufficient distance to guarantee the end result.

Potter was an Alaska Highway worker and a United States veteran of World War I. He was described as a "massive" man — over six feet tall and weighing more than 220 pounds. In July 1945, he stabbed to death Mrs. Edna Ina Rogers in Dawson Creek. At 6:00 a.m. on January 10, he was brought into the South Wing Gallows with his hands tied behind his back. A minister read the Lord's Prayer while Ellis bound the man's feet and then placed the noose and hood over his head. In the basement the prison surgeon waited, stethoscope in hand, to determine the moment of death. Ellis then pulled the trap door lever which sent the doomed man plummeting downwards. But he had miscalculated the weight of the man. When the noose tightened, as the rope reached its full length, the force generated by the body's free fall was so great that the noose completely severed his neck. The decapitated body fell to the floor below.

News of the gory event was not made public until the following day when the deceased's legal counsel, Thomas Hurley, brought the story to the press. "It is revolting to me and I am supposed to be tougher than the ordinary man and woman who are not mixed up with crime or hangings," he said. The following day Attorney-General Maitland announced that there would be a full enquiry into the beheading. He added: "The accident was apparently a result of a miscalculation or error of judgment by the hangman."[5] Despite the incident, John Ellis continued to conduct the hangings at Oakalla until 1950, when he retired and was replaced by Camille Branchaud of Montreal.

Medos and Houston Die

Just before noon on February 26, 1947, a Vancouver Police detective was tipped-off that four men had donned masks and looked as though they were about to pull an armed robbery at the Royal Bank on the corner of Renfrew and First. Police cars were immediately dispatched to the area, but by the time they arrived the suspects had fled, without doing the hold up. As officers began to comb the streets, Constable Smith spotted the four men in a stolen car at First and Main. The officer tried to ram the suspect car with the police cruiser, but they managed to dodge out of the way by driving up on the sidewalk. By the time the officer turned his car around the suspects were out of sight. Five minutes later the stolen car was found abandoned in the 2300 block of Kitchener Street. Once again police swarmed down into the area. One of the first officers on the scene, Detective Percy Hoare, asked three nearby school children if they had seen any suspicious-looking men. One the lads had observed the men get out of the car and run in the direction of the city dump on the False Creek flats. The boy agreed to climb into the police car and show the detective where he saw the men run.

Speeding towards the garbage dump, Detective Hoare got on the police radio and advised other units where the suspects were heading. Plain-clothes Prowler Officers Charles Boyes and George Oliver Ledingham responded to the call. The officers spotted three young men casually walking along the railway tracks near the Great Northern Roundhouse and decided to check them out. The officers got out of their car near the roundhouse and started after the men. As the officers were approaching the suspects, Detective Hoare and his passenger came up to the scene. Later he recalled the deadly progression of events:

> The three men kept walking casually and never made a move as the officers rushed towards them. Then I saw them stop. Boyes and Ledingham talked to them and showed them their badges. All five men turned and started walking toward me. As they came closer I said: "Who are you fellows?" They didn't answer. I looked down and saw something black hanging from the tall man's (Carter's) belt. I grabbed it and it was an automatic.
>
> One of the others stepped back and shot the policeman next to him. I don't know which officer it was. I dropped to the ground and the men fired three shots at me. One of them got me as I fell. The one I took the gun away from started to run and I let him have it with my gun. The automatic had dropped to the ground. I think I winged him. Then I got him again and he went down.[6]

In a few violent seconds a flurry of sixteen shots had been fired and three men lay dead. Constables Boyes and Ledingham never had a chance to defend themselves. While Detective Hoare was struggling with Douglas Carter, Harry Medos and William Henderson stepped back and opened fire on the constables. They fell to the tracks, critically wounded. Both were dead upon arrival at the hospital.

Although Detective Hoare had been shot twice, bullets penetrating his hip and shoulder, he was able to return fire. He hit Carter twice, killing him. The four remaining rounds in his revolver were spent in the direction of Medos and Henderson as they escaped. One bullet struck Medos in the buttocks.

In search of a vehicle, the fugitives came across a truck belonging to Mr. M. Chapotelle. Medos, now bleeding profusely, got into the truck and attempted to start it. Chapotelle's sixteen-year-old son Andrew saw the man trying to steal the vehicle and informed his father. When the middle-aged man confronted Medos he was met with the following response: "Come on. Help me get this thing started or I'll blow your brains out!" Medos then pointed his weapon at the owner's head. Instead of assisting him, Chapotelle slammed the truck door in the suspect's face and ran into a nearby building where he phoned the police. Within a minute several officers arrived and were hot on the fugitive's trail. They followed patches of blood to a vacant lot and then to a house on East Sixth Avenue. In the basement they arrested 17-year-old William Henderson and 19-year-old Harry Medos, who was now faint from loss of blood. Medos was rushed to Vancouver General Hospital and underwent emergency surgery. Several months later he and Henderson were convicted of the slayings. Henderson received a life sentence, because of his age, and Medos was sentenced to death.

October 1, 1947, was the day on which Harry Medos would expiate his crime by hanging on Oakalla's gallows. He was not to die alone. Davis Houston, a 28-year-old Native Indian, who had won two appeals against his conviction for the bludgeon murder of Beatrice Smith, at a Belize Inlet logging camp, was scheduled to hang on the same day. At 5:00 a.m., only an hour before the hanging, Medos complained to the guard on Death Row that he had a headache and wanted an aspirin. Appreciating the strain the young man must have been going through, the guard agreed to get him some medication. Once the officer was off the tier, Medos took out a razor blade he had stashed under the mattress and methodically slashed his wrists. Several minutes later the officer returned and found the inmate lying very still on his cell bed. At first he thought Medos was dead, but when he and another guard entered the cell, they found that he was conscious and had lost only a small quantity of blood as most of it had congealed and created a clot. The prison physician bandaged his wrists and declared him fit for execution.

Less than an hour after the failed suicide attempt, Medos and Houston were brought into the execution chamber. Besides the usual witnesses, press reporters, and prison officials, many police officers were on hand to witness the death of the man who had been responsible for slaying two of their fellow members. John Ellis conducted the execution, and at exactly 6:06 a.m. both men were pronounced dead.

Mass Escape
During Oakalla's first two decades there was virtually no segregation of juvenile and first offenders from other prisoners. In the early 1930s local community groups began to petition for a separate institution for youths, claiming that Oakalla was little more than a "School for Crime." In 1934, Rev. J.D. Hobden, Executive Secretary of the John Howard Society, successfully urged the provincial government to initiate an experimental project at Oakalla whereby first offenders would be segregated from other criminals. Calling themselves the "Gazoonie Gang," and later the "Star Class," these inmates were isolated from the rest of the prison on the top two tiers of the West Wing. They were provided with special workshops, training, and privileges. For example, they were not locked in their cells during meal periods like other sentenced prisoners.

November 30, 1947 was a cold and miserable day. A winter fog had crept up from Deer Lake and blanketed the entire prison. On tier 5-Left, eighteen Star Class youths between the ages of fifteen to twenty-one were getting ready for supper. Allan Todd, 17, a street-smart kid who grew up on the streets of East Vancouver, and Eddy Mason, a dopey-eyed young man, who looked much older than eighteen, were the tier leaders. Supper had been served by six, and staff had visually checked on the youths twenty minutes later. After the guards left, Mason went into his cell and retrieved a foot-long piece of bandsaw which another inmate had smuggled out of the woodwork shop. He walked over to the window at the far end of the tier and diligently cut through the last few millimetres of metal holding the bars in place. He had been using the same tactic of packing soap to conceal the cut bars employed by Bagley when he fled the West Wing more than fifteen years earlier.

Once Mason had removed the bars, he and Todd tied several sheets to the frame, asked some of their friends to join them, and then climbed down the side of the prison wall and disappeared in the heavy fog. Once the others realized that the first two had safely made it off-grounds without being noticed, twelve more young offenders could not resist the temptation of freedom, and they too scaled down the rope and made their way over the fence along Royal Oak Avenue.

These fourteen young men had just pulled off the largest prison break in Canadian penal history. This figure would never be matched at Oakalla, although there were several occasions when the record was threatened.

The break-out was not discovered until staff made their next rounds half an hour later. Almost as soon as the call of the escape went out, a small crime-wave raced through Burnaby and the surrounding area. Within hours of the break, several break-and-enters, thefts (primarily of civilian clothes), and stolen automobiles were reported.

Within a couple of hours, escapees Frank Cross, 17, and Tom McKeller, 16, who had just been transferred to Oakalla from the Boys' Industrial School in Coquitlam, were nabbed by police after a short foot chase down the north lane of Pender at Boundary Road. About a block from there, police also discovered fifteen-year-old Donald Goudie trying to "hot wire" a car. The three fugitives were picked up without a struggle. Later that Saturday night, Vancouver police spotted and arrested Edward Jones and his older friend Donald Walker in front of the YMCA on Burrard Street. Early the next day, Robert Dickie and Edwin Tancowny were flushed out at the Tancowny residence at 3959 Douglas Street in Burnaby. Fifteen-year-old Dickie said, "It was fun while it lasted." Thus after two full days, half of the fugitives were back in custody.

When Todd and Mason escaped they hooked up with twenty-year-old William Drader. The three young men met up with friends in East Vancouver and were able to get a handgun and some cash. They planned to head to California for the winter. Finding a vehicle was no problem, they stole an unmarked Vancouver Police cruiser from the city yards and headed south, only receiving a routine check at the border. After four days, and several break-ins, the fugitives had made their way to The Dalles, a small resort area east of Portland along the Columbia River. Here they broke into another garage, but the local police were alerted and, when a unit arrived, Mason rounded a corner and ran into the arms of an officer. Todd and Drader fled on foot and hopped a train that was heading east. About fifty miles later, near the town of Arlington, the boys jumped from the train and ran into the hills. But a posse was hot on their trail and picked them up after an eight hour search. Todd was found with a loaded .25 calibre automatic in his waistband.

Two days later, Jack Richardson and Robert Davis were arrested in Mission after a wild car chase through the Fraser Valley. The final two escapees, Maurice Sicotte and James Allison, were apprehended December 9. They had been hiding in a log cabin on the north shore of Burrard Inlet, making trips into Vancouver at night in a stolen rowboat. In the wake of the escape, two guards were fired for negligence, five additional officers were hired to increase security, and the Attorney-General announced that the Warden had been given full power to implement any changes necessary to see that the "rigid system of discipline" was enforced.

Millman continued to have faith in these young offenders and refused to have them locked down during meal breaks. On New Year's Day, 1949, another eight members of the Star Class took advantage of Millman's decision and escaped from the West Wing by sawing through the tier-window bars, as before. Five were almost immediately picked up by the Burnaby Police. They were found hanging around the Industrial School for Girls, trying to send their "girlfriends" some cigarettes they had just stolen in a coffee shop break-in.

The Inmates Revolt

Although tension was growing within the prison, the outside world still considered Oakalla an orderly and regimented institution. On January 31, 1948, the facade crumbled. That evening all sixty South Wing inmates refused to eat dinner and started a disturbance.

Prior to the incident, the remanded South Wing prisoners had been complaining of the quality of food and living conditions. In a six-page letter "smuggled" out of the prison to a federal Member of Parliament, an inmate made the following allegations: "The way the food is put up is disgraceful... the stew is generally cold with a film of grease on top of it... it is slopped on trays like it is being fed to a bunch of pigs, the spaghetti runs in with the prunes." The inmate went on to complain about the washing of the trays. "The used trays are given a dip in lukewarm water and are not rinsed. Soap and food particles still cling to them. You can taste soap in most of the food."[7] He also alleged that most of the bedding was infested with lice, and prisoners were rarely given the opportunity to bathe.

At first the inmates stayed in their cells, shouting and threatening destruction. But their cell-doors were not locked, and some of the prisoners went onto the tiers and banged their metal cups on the bars, and threw trays at the windows. Officers from other wings were summoned to lock the unit down. Some force was required, but there were no reports of injuries. At least thirty windows had been smashed during the demonstration and seven inmates, who had been observed breaking them, were brought into Warden's Court the next morning. They were punished with up to ten strokes of the paddle. Partly to protest the paddling, the food strike continued on for several more days.

When word of the incident reached the public there were calls for an open inquiry into the inmate's allegations. Recalling how his predecessor had dispelled previous reports of poor living conditions, Warden Millman allowed a *Vancouver Sun* reporter to tour the prison and conduct his own investigation. The reporter found that the bulk of complaints were unjustified. Oakalla was kept clean, all bedding was sufficiently laundered, the food trays were washed with steam and boiling water, and, in the reporter's opinion, he considered the food to be better than any other penal institution in Canada. He also stated that discipline at Oakalla, security apart, was probably less stringent than at any military barrack.[8]

Prestyko's Strange Request

Occasionally condemned men made last requests that others found strange or unusual. None was more bizarre than the one made by Walter Prestyko. He and William Worobec were convicted of the double murder of an elderly man and his wife in their Vancouver home in June 1949. The two men were to be hanged together at Oakalla on February 28, 1950.

At 6:00 a.m. that day, Prestyko was the first to be ushered into the hushed execution chamber. With an officer at each side, he was brought onto the trap door. The executioner quickly buckled leather straps around his ankles and then put the noose over his head, with the knot just off the left ear. But when John Ellis began to place the black hood over Prestyko's head, the inmate attempted to turn his head away. Prestyko looked at the hangman and asked, "Do I have to have it?" Ellis insisted and Prestyko eventually complied. Seconds later his partner in crime entered the room. Worobec showed no emotion as Ellis prepared for the execution. At 6:03 a.m. the lever was released and both men dropped to their deaths.

After the hanging, a guard who had been with Prestyko during the previous night explained that the reason he asked that the hood not be placed over his head was that Prestyko wanted to watch Worobec die with him. The headlines of a local newspaper that day read: "'I Want To See Him Hang' Slayer's Last Request."[9]

Another significant aspect of this hanging was the reaction of the Sheriff's Department to newspaper accounts of the deaths. In mid-March, the Sheriff's Department issued a statement declaring reporters were to be banned from all further hangings at Oakalla. This was in response to what they referred to as "the printing of distasteful stories." One newspaper had described the Coroner's Jury viewing the contorted shape of the deceaseds' necks.

Frank Cotton, Sheriff of the County of Westminster, who supervised all aspects of Oakalla executions, made the following statement:

> It is my point of view that the law changed hangings
> from something public to something private. Word

In 1948 prisoners revolted over unsanitary conditions in the kitchen.

pictures in the newspaper of the execution are making
executions more public than ever. I understand the only
persons I may not bar from an execution are ministers
of the gospel, justices of the peace and relatives of the
condemned person.[10]

Less than five months later, just prior to the execution of Frederick
Ducharme, the Sheriff's declaration was overturned by the Attorney-
General's Department. Cotton was advised that, although the Criminal
Code stated that he had control over who should be allowed to attend
hangings, the press still had an obligation to inform the public of
executions, and therefore must be permitted to witness them.

Frederick Ducharme Hanged
At about 7:30 a.m. on November 9, 1949, the body of Ferne Blanche
Fisher was found floating in the water beneath a railway trestle in
False Creek. The attractive 45-year-old single woman had been a
dress fitter at the downtown Woodward's Department Store. She
had last been seen alive standing in front of a local movie theatre,
early in the evening of the night before. Her body was clad only in
a coat, a dress, and a slip stained with blood. She had apparently
been sexually assaulted prior to her death, and, at some point, her

pubic hair had been shaven. The following day, Chief Constable Mulligan issued a warning that there was probably a "sex maniac" loose on the streets of Vancouver. Several days later, the Coroner's Jury concluded that Ferne Fisher died from drowning, although her internal and external injuries, including extensive bruising around her neck, may have contributed to her death.

On December 5, Frederick Roger Ducharme was arrested in Vancouver by two rookie police officers for exposing himself in public. The 28-year-old red-haired Frenchman was caught wearing only a "raincoat, rubber boots, woman's scarf and a silk shirt."[11] Ducharme possessed a sexual abnormality. The police reported that, at the time of his arrest, he had strapped his fourteen-inch penis to his chest with boot laces.[12] The slightly retarded man had a history of arrests for exposing himself in public. While in custody for the above offence, he was charged with the murder of Miss Fisher.

By the time of his trial in early March 1950, a great deal of media hype and public curiosity had built up. People lined up early to get a seat in the courtroom, which would be crammed with spectators hoping that Ducharme would testify. After several days, the courtroom became more like a circus ring than a trial setting as the sensational testimony of witnesses kept the spectators on the edge of their seats. Evidence brought forward revealed more startling deviations of the accused. He was said to have collected more than fifty women's lingerie items, which he kept in his home.

During the trial, Ducharme admitted to having been with Ferne Fisher on the night of her death. He stated that he saw her standing in front of the Rio Theatre and asked her if she wanted a ride home in his car. He said she voluntarily got in, and after driving around for a while he took her down to the sawdust piles at False Creek where they parked. Once in the back seat of the car, he testified that he attempted to have intercourse with her:

> Suddenly she got hysterical and started to hit me. So I grabbed her throat to keep her from yelling. She took my arm away so I grabbed her wrists. She broke away and scratched my face and hit me on the back of the neck. By this time I was mad and my temper was high. She got out of the car, but not stopping to pick up things and ran on to the bridge...[13]

Ducharme went on to contend that Miss Fisher then jumped off the bridge and into False Creek, committing suicide. The Crown argued that after the rape in the car, Ducharme took the woman, who was either unconscious or still fighting, and murdered her by throwing

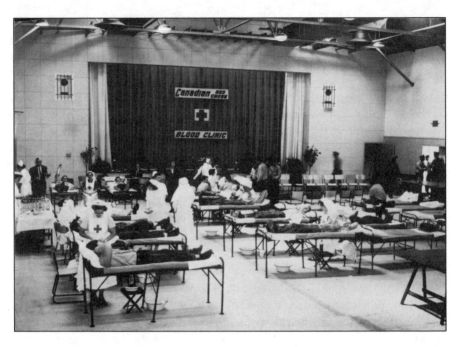

Prisoners donating blood to Canadian Red Cross.

her off the bridge. After seventeen days of testimony and physical evidence, Ducharme was found guilty of murder. His trial had been the longest murder trial in British Columbia's legal history.

Although originally sentenced to hang on June 30, Ducharme was finally brought before Oakalla's gallows at 6:00 a.m. on July 14, 1950, after a series of unsuccessful last-minute appeals. He went to his death, pronounced at 6:18 a.m. by the prison doctor, without any sign of emotion. As in his life, so in his death, Ducharme was shadowed by mystery. His body was claimed by an unknown person, described only as a "friend," and his burial place and time were kept secret.

Commission Investigates Oakalla

After the near-riot in 1948, reports of deplorable conditions and overcrowding within Oakalla continued to be leaked to the media. By 1950, public pressure to investigate these allegations had become so strong that the provincial government decided to launch a full inquiry. On May 5, a commission was established "to enquire into and report upon the state and management of the gaols of the Province, with special reference to the overcrowded condition of Oakalla."[14]

What investigators discovered was that there had been no significant development in the Provincial Gaol System since the construction

The Young Offenders' Unit.

of Oakalla in 1912. However, recent literature in penology called for prisons to be more like "treatment" centres than places of punishment. The new ideology assumed that the inmate was sick: physically, mentally, or socially. The prisoner's offence was a "manifestation or symptom of his illness, a cry for help... early and accurate diagnosis, followed by prompt and effective therapeutic interventions, assured an affirmative prognosis — rehabilitation."[15] This was the foundation for the new "Medical Model" approach to corrections.

The commission found that although other jurisdictions had begun to focus on attempting to rehabilitate the offender, Oakalla was too overcrowded, and lacked the facilities for providing medical training and resources, to carry out any such program. They also reported that, in Oakalla, "hard labour seems to be a misnomer, for, although there is a certain amount of labour done, it is not hard work, and in many cases prisoners do not work at all."[16]

When the report was made public the provincial government claimed that it would immediately take measures to implement these recommendations fully. The rehabilitation of offenders became the new goal of penology in the province, and Oakalla was to be at the forefront.

The first step in this new direction began on February 26, 1951, when twenty-one youths (between the ages of 16 and 23) were admitted to the newly constructed Young Offenders' Unit. Situated down the hill from the Main Gaol, the cellblock had accommodation for 100 prisoners, its own kitchen facilities, and modern training shops in the basement for woodwork and diesel and motor mechanics.

During the late 1940s Warden Millman had made a number of cosmetic improvements to the appearance of Oakalla by purchasing a tractor for landscaping, and hiring a painter-guard to supervise the repainting of almost every building on the grounds. The exterior of Oakalla was spruced up — but inside its walls, trouble was brewing. The population had continued to rise, reaching 900 by 1949. Not enough guards were hired to maintain the previous inmate-guard ratio, which resulted in decreased security and observation. The rampage in 1948 was only a foreshadowing of the real turmoil that existed in the cramped men's units. While the new prison for young offenders had brought about a number of improvements for them, virtually no changes had been initiated for the adults. Millman was ready to retire, and the government sought to start anew by bringing in someone who could bring reform to Oakalla by jumping on the "Medical Model" band wagon.

Five

The "Rehabilitation Era" 1952-1963

Hugh Graham Christie was the government's choice to bring Oakalla into the new era of rehabilitation. Attorney-General Wismer stated he believed the 38-year-old former Director of Corrections in Saskatchewan would, "give impetus to the government's program of prisoner rehabilitation at Oakalla".[1] Unlike previous wardens, Christie had not worked his way to the top through the ranks of the Provincial Police Force (which was disbanded in 1951 when the RCMP took over most jurisdictions). His background was social work.

When Christie took over the prison in July 1952, he was confronted by some of the worst gaol conditions in Canada. Two major problems confronted him: the trustee system and overcrowding.

The trustie system had been in use at Oakalla since it opened in 1912, but by 1952 it was out of control and these inmates, not the guards, ran some areas of the prison. Trusties were "trusted" prisoners who moved about freely throughout parts of the prison, without direct supervision, so that they could perform tasks such as mopping and sweeping floors and running errands. Each passing year saw fewer and fewer staff available to watch over the expanding population, while more prisoners were left on their own to carry out duties. The inmates soon took advantage of the situation and a drug smuggling operation was organized by the trusties. Instead of them being the most trustworthy, they were now the "heavies," the ones with the most power. By 1952, there were nearly 100 trustie positions.

Christie slashed the number of unsupervised inmates to about a dozen. He also waged a war on the drug epidemic by segregating all convicts who had been labelled "addicts" to one section of the East Wing. The Warden wanted to bring about reform and new programs for the prisoners, but first he wanted to restore the authority of the guards over their charges, which had been lost during the previous decade.

However, prison overcrowding was out of Christie's hands. Until funds could be allocated for the construction of new buildings, he could do little but sit back and watch the population swell. In 1950, there were 460 cells for male prisoners yet the actual count averaged out at almost double that — more than 800 per day. Accommodation was made by placing two men per cell in the top two tiers of the West and East Wings, crowding the sick and elderly into a central tower, and housing less security-risk prisoners in the wooden Old Gaol. Two years later, the count had passed 900, and double bunk beds were also placed in the South Wing. Although there had been some opposition in the other units, the South Wing inmates responded with greater hostility. They believed that since they were waiting trial, and presumed innocent, they deserved greater freedoms than the sentenced population.

The problems of overcrowding were coupled with an acute shortage of officers. In late 1952, there was one officer for every seven or eight inmates; Christie believed that a good institution would have one guard for every two or three prisoners.

The staff loved him, and the prisoners hated him. He was trying to give back something to the officers that the cons had taken away; but it wasn't going to be easy. The former trustees were furious over their loss of power and benefits from the drug trade. The addicts were going through painful withdrawal; the flow of their contraband had been reduced to a trickle. The South Wing had their beefs too. By late September 1952, Oakalla was a powder keg. Christie could feel the tension and informed the provincial government that a riot was near. Prior to coming to Oakalla he had observed conditions that led to prison riots in Eastern Canada and was now seeing the same thing here. "It is reasonable to expect similar outbreaks here," he warned.[2] A week later vigilant guards in the South Wing thwarted a mass escape when they discovered cut metal bars at the far end of one of the corridors. It was the final straw; eight days later the fury of a full-scale riot was unleashed.

Riot Erupts

On the morning of October 2, 1952, several inmates in the South Wing decided to damage the double bunk beds which had recently been installed in their cells. This was done quietly and not noticed until one of the guards was doing a tier-check. For some reason the staff decided not to investigate the mischief; they simply called in one of the guard-tradesmen to repair the beds. While they were being repaired, a scheduled period of exercise in the outdoor South Wing yard was allowed to proceed. Nearly ninety men went out for fresh air. At approximately 10:15 a.m. the prisoners were called to return to their cells.

In the wing, two staff were assigned to provide supervision. During the exercise period one officer was stationed in a tower which overlooked the yard. The second guard, Officer Burns, was inside the unit with the guard-tradesman, Officer Peek. As soon as the inmates filed back into the wing, they began to take it over. They barricaded the main entrance which led from the wing to Centre Hall, grabbing anything they could get their hands on: benches, chairs, garbage cans, and metal beds ripped from the walls of their cells. Within minutes Christie had been notified of the disturbance. He later told reporters:

> On the first report of trouble, I got four or five guards together in the centre hall and tried to push the door into the south wing open. It gave a little and we tried to force it further with levers.
> Had I been able to get in then I think we could have handled the situation properly. But by this time they had the barricade jammed up to the ceiling.[3]

While some of the prisoners reinforced the barricade, many others went on a rampage trashing their cells and smashing out windows with pieces of porcelain from sinks and toilets. They gathered the debris and stockpiled it, waiting to fire it when staff stormed the wing. Some of them set mattresses ablaze and toxic smoke spread throughout the cellblock.

In a show of support for their fellow prisoners, the West Wing began to rattle bars and shout along with the others. Fortunately, they were locked in their cells and could not do much damage to the unit itself. They did manage to break twenty toilets and sinks, and torch one

Oct. 3, 1952. RCMP stand by while guards douse South Wing during Oakalla's first riot.

mattress. In the East Wing, the convicted drug addicts, who had been segregated to one side of the wing, were able to put the locking mechanisms for their cells out of commission. Female prisoners from the nearby Women's Gaol could hear the rebellion, and a group of them barricaded themselves in a recreation room, and smashed furniture, a piano, and more than two hundred panes of glass.

Caught in the middle of a full-blown riot, the Warden took immediate action:

> All outside gangs were called in and locked in their cells. A semi-circle of six riflemen was placed around the outside of the South Wing cell block as a precautionary measure. I called the R.C.M.P. and asked for twelve riflemen to reinforce these men lined outside

around the cell block as an additional precaution in case the outside bars were forced. Fourteen men and an N.C.O. were immediately supplied. The penitentiary was contacted for the loan of their riot gun and tear gas shells which they agreed to send over for us as long as their men would not be implicated in any way. The acetylene unit was brought up from the motor mechanics shop preparatory to cutting out the South Wing gate which swung in and therefore had to be cut with the torch to be removed. The fire hoses were connected and tested and 2x4's were brought in to act as levers on the debris at the gate.[4]

The prison's fire hoses proved to be rotten and split, so the Burnaby Fire Department was brought in. All on and off-duty guards were summoned to the prison. Within a few hours a force of one hundred men had assembled to retake the South Wing. Several officers manned the fire hoses and flooded the inside of the unit with water, putting an end to the fires that had been set. Another officer was deployed with a gas gun to the northeast corner of the Wing. The remainder assembled in Centre Hall, ready to move in as soon as the barricade was removed.

Christie then reached the barricaded prisoners by telephone and spoke to the leaders. He also talked to the two officers trapped in the South Wing and was assured that their lives were not threatened. The inmates had no beefs with the officers, and — contrary to newspaper reports — the pair were not held as hostages. Christie spoke to the inmates for some time, but they wanted to see him in person. To appease them, he walked around to the outside of the South Wing and carried on his conversation by talking to them through the broken windows. The prisoners demanded: No more than one man per cell; use of the East or West Wing exercise yards (the South Wing yard was one-third the size); visits with women other than their wives or relatives in the Women's Gaol; and no reprisals for the damage to the cellblock.

The Warden refused every demand. He had no alternative but to double-bunk some cells; segregation of exercise yards had to be enforced to prevent drug trafficking, as the remand population was always in and out of court; and the men could not be allowed to have visits from just any women, especially the younger ones, to keep the "hardened criminals from recruiting molls and prostitutes."[5]

Christie expressed sympathy regarding the overcrowding problem, but pointed out, if he started to make concessions, they would see violence as a means of obtaining goals. The Warden then gave them one last chance to end their siege peacefully. When they refused, he gave the order to retake the prison.

The officer standing outside with the gas gun volleyed tear-gas shells through the windows and into the Wing. At the same time, officers in Centre Hall removed the gate with the acetylene torch and within minutes had dismantled the barricade. Gas masks were in limited supply, so the majority of the guards found themselves in the same situation as the inmates — overcome by fumes. Several guards carried fire hoses into the wing and were successful in forcing the inmates away from the entrance. However, the officers quickly found themselves trapped on the bottom floor. All of the prisoners had run up the flights of stairs to the tiers above and began pelting the guards with large pieces of porcelain whenever they approached the stairs.

One of the senior guards, Dick Bready, decided enough was enough. He grabbed an inhalator and another tear gas gun and charged the stairs amidst a deluge of flying steel and rubble. When he reached the second landing he began to fire gas shells at the feet of the convicts who retreated to the third floor. Bready and the other officers followed behind, and as prisoners attempted to escape the powerful vapors, the staff herded the unruly felons onto the tiers and into cells. Within minutes the remaining prisoners, eyes burning and clothing soaked, meekly surrendered.

Although Bready's actions were incredibly dangerous, single-handedly he had virtually put an end to the uprising. The following day, he was hailed as a "hero" in the press.

The disturbance had ended at about 2:30 p.m., only four hours after it began. However, the rebellious group had, at that time, caused the worst prison riot in British Columbia's history.

Not only was the revolt quickly put to an end, but the Warden decided to immediately hold "Disciplinary Court." Of the ninety inmates housed in the South Wing, twenty-five were deemed to be uninvolved and were sent to the dormitory in the hospital tower. Most of the remaining received reprimands and other minor punishments. However, twenty-five of the most aggressive South and West Wing rioters were brought before the Warden and whipped with a leather strap. Although Christie was a leader in correctional reform, he felt that he had no alternative but to use the paddle. He later told reporters, "I don't like punishment, but it must be certain, immediate and decisive when used.... Many people have tried to change prisons by wiping out the punitive approach in the hope of instituting modern treatment. But they have failed because they have taken away the punishment before they had the modern system set up."[6]

At 8:00 p.m. the sixty-five offenders who remained in the South Wing were bedded down for the night, dormitory style, on the bottom floors. The inmates each received four blankets, however, the unit was very damp and the cold October wind howled through the broken windows all night. The following day clean up began and repairs to the cells commenced.

In Hugh Christie's subsequent report to the Inspector of Gaols, he took partial responsibility for the turmoil within the prison. He had taken over the position only three months before the riot and had attempted to eradicate a number of serious problems that were plaguing the gaol. In the conclusion of the report he stated:

> As reported to members of the Commission, I have, in the three months I have been here, seen as much drug traffic, theft of government goods, gambling, homosexuality, drunkenness, bribery, pay-offs, intimidation, brutality, and indiscriminate mixing of youth and degeneracy, as I have seen in any penal institution. The seasoned criminal likes this sort of setting to ply his trade and will control the prison for you in return for his profit. To allow this to continue is to make the work of running the prison an easy one. To do as much as can be done to rectify this situation with or without the adequate resources, is the reason I accepted a job as Warden at Oakalla.[7]

Following the riot, Christie was instructed by Robert Bonner, Attorney-General of the newly elected Social Credit Government, to open Oakalla to a representative of the media so that the existing conditions could be made public. *Province* reporter Bruce Larsen was contacted by Christie and given free access to the prison for four days. Several days later, the newspaper's front-page headline read: "Oakalla's Disgrace Laid Bare: Finishing School of Crime." The two-page story attacked every aspect of Oakalla, indicating how poor the prison had become since the last time it was toured by the media. Attorney-General Bonner stated that through the government's new commitment to rehabilitation, these conditions would be rectified.

Attempting to Reform

Christie's first initiative in penal reform was to hire a complement of fifty more officers. This alone eliminated the need for an inmate trustie system. He also upgraded recruiting requirements. "There is no point in recruiting a cow," he said. "We have to have men with higher than average intelligence. Anyone just average will find himself being outwitted by the inmates. Then he gets vicious and abuses his authority."[8]

In 1953, Westgate, a single-level, 400-cell unit, was built alongside Royal Oak Avenue. The unit had some advantages over the Main Gaol. It was generally quieter than the stacked tiers of the Main Gaol; and its wide-open tiers allowed for group (therapy) discussions, unlike the Main Gaol tiers, which were barely wide enough for one person to stand. By 1955, Westgate had become responsible for the total management of the farm, the dairy, fourteen industrial shops, and seventeen work gangs. The prisoners' motto was: "work hard, play hard, and study hard." It became a standing joke that whenever a guard mentioned "Westgate," he would place his hand across his heart and thank the Lord.

In the same year, Oakalla's most cherished work-project began when fourteen Clydesdale draft horses were brought to work the farm and plough the fields. The first team of Bay Geldings, harnesses, and two wagons were purchased from the Worthington Estate. Mrs. Worthington wanted a good home for her horses. All their grooming and nourishing was undertaken by inmates, who took great pride in

Westgate Unit.

70

Oakalla's pride and joy. The Clydesdale horses.

watching the sturdy beasts parade around the property.

Christie believed that the reform of inmates could also be affected by improving the punishment facilities. The condemned dirt-floored isolation chambers beneath the central portion of the Old Gaol were finally closed in 1954, when the basement of one of the cow barns was reconstructed and converted into the new Segregation Unit. Twelve of its twenty-eight cells were called "Quiet Cells," or "Dark Cells." The cells were each enclosed by a thick wooden door which muffled the level of disruption caused by unruly convicts. There was also one cell which contained iron rings which were fastened to the floor. Uncontrollably violent prisoners could be strapped spread-eagle to the floor to prevent them from injuring themselves or others. The use of this cell was phased out after a few years when the hospital was equipped with a padded cell.

The philosophy behind the "rehabilitation" approach was the "Medical Model." Therefore, paralleling major expansions in labour programs were developments in the medical and mental health fields. Christie began by hiring a full-time medical officer. In 1952 Dr. Guy Richmond was appointed Senior Medical Officer. When he started, medical facilities at Oakalla were in shambles. The hospital was located in the center of the Main Gaol, on the top two floors. There

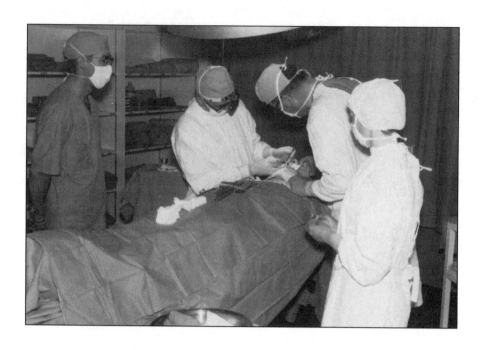

More than 600 plastic surgery operations were performed at Oakalla.

was almost no segregation of addicts going through withdrawal, the mentally ill, and prisoners with tuberculosis. Only minor ailments could be treated.

Richmond purchased medical equipment, and converted an office into an operating room for minor surgery. For the first few years, he had to make do with a wooden kitchen table as his operating table. Shortly thereafter, Dr. Richmond was approached by Dr. Edward Lewison, a plastic surgeon, who wished to conduct experiments on inmates to see whether the altering of unsightly features, such as correcting a crooked nose, could have any rehabilitative effect. Dr. Lewison offered his services without fee, and prison authorities allowed him to proceed. He started out doing basic rhinoplasty operations but was soon reshaping jaws and ears, and removing squints, scars, tattoos, and other deformities that he believed led to feelings of inferiority and delinquency. Over fifteen years, Dr. Lewison carried out more than 600 operations on Oakalla's offenders. It appears the success of such operations in reducing recidivism rates was never documented. However, as Dr. Richmond once stated: "His patients are most grateful and cannot but be assisted thereby toward social adjustment, however slow their progress."[9]

In 1953, Oakalla's Consulting Psychiatrist, Dr. Ernest Campbell, was given approval by the Corrections Branch to begin electro-convulsive or "shock" therapy on prisoners. Dr. Richmond once commented:

> We have employed both major and minor shock-therapy, and find that in the agitated and depressed individual the results have exceeded our expectations... With the anticipated increase of psychiatric resources in this Gaol, it is hoped that an increasing number of inmates may receive treatment of this nature.[10]

Shock-therapy was permanently suspended in August 1954, following the death of Dr. Campbell.

Only three years after the riot, Christie again opened Oakalla to the press. During that time he had doubled the staff to 300 from 150; constructed new facilities that reduced overcrowding and provided segregation; initiated medical and other "treatment" programs; and, as he put it, "changed the atmosphere" within the prison:

> When I came here the East Wing used to run the prison. The East Wing houses the hardened criminals, drug addicts — "the real cons." I took over from them and they didn't like it. We had one riot. Two Christmases ago we were as close to another riot as I ever want to be. But they're beaten now and they know it. They don't like me. But they respect me. They do what I say.[11]

After the riot, the prison had been labelled one of the nation's worst; now it was cited as one of the best. Although there was little concrete data to show how effective medical experiments and the like had been in rehabilitating offenders, if nothing else, most of these initiatives had vastly improved the overall condition of the prison and reduced tension. However, in the first few years following the riot, Christie had faced only minor disruptions and the rehabilitation programs had proceeded without any crises. It wouldn't take long before his brilliant record was tarnished.

Christie's Demon

As warden, one of Christie's most difficult responsibilities was having to preside over all of British Columbia's sentences of execution. He was opposed to capital punishment, and the first hangings at which he officiated were so upsetting they gave him

Warden Hugh Christie.

ulcers. "It is completely out of harmony with our rehabilitation program," he once said. "I want it removed from Oakalla. An execution disturbs the entire prison population. Even good staff find it tough to take part in a hanging."[12] The first hanging he witnessed at Oakalla was of 60-year-old Arthur Cunningham. This individual's violent personality was so appalling that, even though the Warden didn't think so, many others felt capital punishment was a suitable sentence.

Most convicted men who went to the Oakalla gallows were repentant, sorrowful, and accepted spiritual counselling. Others maintained their innocence, were atheists, or faced execution with silent defiance. Only Arthur Cunningham went to his death vowing that, given the opportunity, he would certainly kill again.

In 1941 he was acquitted of a murder charge. In 1952, he had pleaded guilty to murdering a farmer near Prince Rupert to rob him of forty dollars. At the sentencing hearing he also bragged to the judge that he had killed "three or four other men." This guilty plea, to a first-degree murder charge, accepted by the presiding judge, was then believed to be only the second occurrence in Canadian legal history.

The man had lived much of his life as a loner. During his three-month incarceration at Oakalla, the official visitors' record showed only one visitor — and even this was entered by mistake. Early August 5, 1952, only moments before his execution, he made a chilling comment to one of the guards: "Sure I committed murder, and I'd do it again for your pay cheque!"[13]

On January 20, 1953, Alexander Viatkin, 24, who was ailing from advanced stages of tuberculosis, died on the gallows for the murder of an elderly man in an East Vancouver cafe. This execution was the first to be conducted at midnight. Christie said he changed the time of executions from 6:00 a.m. to the stroke of midnight because it was "easier to assemble jurymen at midnight, less disturbance is caused among other inmates, and it avoids the need for cooking meals for guards who have to come in early for dawn hangings."[14]

The Doukhobors

On September 10, 1953, seventy-one women and seventy-seven men were arrested by the RCMP at Perry's Siding in the Slocan Valley. The group belonged to a radical sect of Doukhobor people called the "Sons of Freedom." The Doukhobors were a splinter group of the Russian Orthodox Church that rejected all forms of civil authority. In 1899, seven thousand members emigrated to Canada to escape persecution in Tsarist Russia. After several years, many of the Doukhobors assimilated and accepted Canadian laws. The Sons of Freedom soon emerged, and used public disrobing, arson, and bombing, as a means of "purification" against Doukhobors who accepted government authority, and outsiders who threatened their beliefs.

Charged with contributing to juvenile delinquency and public nudity, these Doukhobors were herded onto a heavily guarded train and transported to Vancouver, then bussed to Oakalla. Authorities had little trouble admitting the offenders and housing them in specially built fire-proof huts. However, when it came time for them to be brought to court, they rebelled. Many put up a fight; others fasted and were too weak to be brought to trial. It took several weeks of combined effort by guards, sheriffs, and court workers, to bring them before a judge. The majority were found guilty and received a variety of provincial and federal sentences. The federally sentenced men were soon transferred from Oakalla; however, the female offenders, who were to be transferred to the B.C. Penitentiary, had to wait at Oakalla until adequate facilities could be provided there.

During this waiting period, the Doukhobor women staged numerous protests and acts of sabotage against the prison. On February 1, 1954, they torched their living quarters. Staff arrived to find the naked women standing in a group, their personal belongings already packed. The women were temporarily moved to the Westgate Unit until a Quonset hut at Oakalla could be rebuilt (at the federal government's expense). Over the next thirty years, Doukhobor prisoners would return to Oakalla, but in much smaller numbers, each time causing problems for the staff by fasting, disrobing, and lighting fires.

Drug Czar Mallock

In late December 1954, Oakalla prison was again confronted with the difficult task of keeping a major player in the criminal underworld within its confines. George Mallock was considered by police to be a kingpin in the Canadian drug trade. In 1951 he had been charged with conspiracy to sell narcotics; however, just before his court date, he jumped $20,000 bail and fled to the United States. Three years later he was arrested by agents of the U.S. Bureau of Narcotics and extradited to Oakalla to await trial.

While in custody he made it known to staff and inmates alike that he would pay five hundred dollars to anyone who could help him escape. Prison officials soon discovered that Mallock also had plans of his own. On a tip received by the RCMP, Christie was informed that someone had better take a good look at Mallock's shoes.

Since Mallock was awaiting trial, he had the privilege of wearing civilian clothes. When he entered the prison, his clothes had undergone special scrutiny, including examination under a fluoroscope metal detector, without raising any suspicions. However, when his dress Oxfords were pried apart, guards were amazed to find four fine jeweler saws and a U.S. ten dollar bill secreted into a cavity in one of the heels. The shoes had been stitched together professionally and were obviously prepared long before Mallock was transferred to Oakalla.

The drug lord made several attempts to escape, in January and February 1955, but all were discovered in their early stages. In March, when he was sentenced to twenty-one to twenty-eight years in the B.C. Penitentiary, he wrote a death threat to Mr. Justice Manson, who had convicted him of the drug charges. In addition, he offered an enticing $2,000 reward to anyone who would aid him in escaping from Oakalla. Security around Mallock was strengthened, and until he was transferred to the penitentiary his every move was closely monitored. For the Warden it was certainly a relief to see him go. Unfortunately only one month later, Christie's luck ran out.

Babcock Skips Church

In contrast to previous violent break-outs, one of the more crafty escapes took place on March 20, 1955. William Babcock, 34, was awaiting transfer to the penitentiary and had just lost an appeal to a twenty-year sentence, with twenty-one strokes of the paddle, for his part in a bank robbery. He, John Bertelsen, and John Waslyenchuk had all been charged with a $28,000 robbery from a Royal Bank in Burnaby, in which shots had been fired by the accused at innocent citizens. With a record of forty-eight convictions spanning fifteen years, Babcock had been described as a "menace to society" by the sentencing judge.

The day before he was to be transferred to the B.C. Penitentiary, Babcock decided to attend a Sunday church service in the centre tower of the Main Gaol. At this particular service twenty-four King's Men, a religious group associated with a local United Church, attended to lead the inmates in song and worship. At the end of the service, Babcock mingled with the group as they packed their musical instruments. He blended in with the civilians, because he was still a South Wing inmate and permitted to wear his own clothes, which happened to be a sharp grey suit. He also managed to somewhat disguise his appearance by wearing a pair of horn-rimmed glasses which belonged to another prisoner (he apparently had a very large nose).

When the rest of the inmates were sent back to their respective units, Babcock stayed with the religious group and went along with them down the stairs into the Centre Hall area. None of the church members said anything when Babcock joined them. Some thought that he was a prison official who was escorting them around; others that he was a new member of their organization. Either way, suspicions were not aroused and the convict walked with them out the front door of the main building. As the men made their way towards the Young Offender's Unit for another service, Babcock split off and waved good-bye, saying he had other matters to attend to.

The officer who had let the church group out the front gate of the Main Gaol then noticed that only twenty-four men had signed in that morning — but he had just counted twenty-five out. At the same time, a guard in the South Wing noticed that Babcock had not returned to his cell. A few minutes later an East Wing guard saw a civilian leave the church group and wander off towards the Cow Barns. The alarm was sounded, and the hunt for the escapee was on. Although nearly 100 guards responded to the breach, the prisoner had obviously planned his escape well in advance, and had a vehicle waiting for him on the outside.

Warden Christie stated that Babcock had made several attempts in the past to escape through impersonation. "Sometimes when he had visitors he would try to impersonate lawyers, members of the John Howard Society or other civilians in the visiting room... but he never got farther than the hall outside the visitors' room."[15] Babcock managed to elude the police for only two months. In May he was arrested by the RCMP in Alert Bay. He had stolen a fishing boat and was making his way up the coast, headed for Alaska.

A Violent Execution

The last thing Christie wanted was for something to go wrong during an execution. In 1955 his fears became a reality.

On September 12, 1953, twelve-year-old Donna Corbett was found in bushes near the Quesnel fair-grounds, strangled to death. A shoelace had been twisted around her neck until she asphyxiated. Carnival worker Lawrence (Corky) Vincent, 25, was charged and eventually convicted of the brutal slaying. He was scheduled to hang at midnight on June 14, 1955.

On the night before his execution, Vincent became very ill and slipped into unconsciousness. Dr. Richmond, the prison physician, transferred the inmate from Death Row to the prison infirmary where he had his stomach pumped. After several hours of intensive observation and medical treatment the condemned man regained consciousness and was sent back to his cell. It is not known what medication or poison Vincent consumed in his suicide attempt. The prison doctor stated that, although it was his practice to administer some sedation to a condemned man a day or two before he was to be hanged, the dosage was in no way strong enough to have caused Vincent's coma.

In the hours leading up to midnight, Vincent's nerves started to unravel and he asked the doctor if he could take something. Fearing that whatever Vincent had taken earlier might not be completely out of his system, Dr. Richmond declined to give the man any further sedatives. Vincent then asked for a shot of alcohol. It was customary for inmates to be allowed to take an ounce or two of brandy before their execution; however, at this time there was none in the jail. Believing that a "therapeutic dosage" might help, the doctor sent a staff member to his home to retrieve a bottle of sherry, and Vincent had a drink. As the hours to midnight dwindled to minutes, Vincent became belligerent. His angry words turned to violence when hangman Camille Branchaud came to his cell to pinion his hands behind his back. As the executioner entered the cell, Vincent lashed out and punched him. The stocky hangman responded by hitting him with the leather bindings. Quickly the inmate was overwhelmed and his arms were tied behind his back. The struggle did not end here for Vincent had to be forcefully dragged to the execution chamber. Once inside the gallows, and in the presence of the witnesses and reporters, the doomed man continued his frenzy. As Branchaud bent over to place the leather bindings around the prisoner's ankles, Vincent thrust his knee into the man's groin. Instinctively the hangman reacted and once again struck the prisoner. Vincent cried out: "Hit me! Hit me! You big fat pig! You yellow rotten pig!"[16]

As the witnesses stood aghast, wondering what was going to happen next, Warden Christie interceded and quietly asked Vincent if he didn't think that a prayer would be more appropriate at a time like this. The criminal replied that he would go when he had made up his mind. The hangman attempted to re-apply the ankle straps, and once again Vincent tried to kick him. For a moment the two men just stood and glared at each other. Finally Vincent agreed to stand still, but he continued to hurl abuse towards Branchaud. "Just whenever you're ready, pig. Just whenever you're ready, pig." As the executioner moved towards him, Vincent spat in his face. As he continued to yell, "Dirty rotten pig. Dirty rotten pig," Branchaud steadily went to work binding his ankles, placing the noose over his head, and finally the black cloth hood. Realizing that the moment of death had now come, Vincent finally stood quietly. Then the trap doors fell open. After the execution a prison official told one reporter: "I've seen forty hangings, and I've never seen anything like this."[17]

Manhunt for Escapees
The embarrassment of the Babcock escape, and horror over the Vincent hanging, were only months old when yet another dramatic escape unfolded. The incident began around 3:00 p.m. on Friday,

79

November 4, when four West Wing inmates entered the unit's exercise yard after having visited family and lawyers in Centre Hall. One of the men was John Wasylenchuk, 40, who had recently received a life sentence for his part in the same robbery as his co-accused partner Babcock. Standing beside Wasylenchuk was Robert Lewis, 24, who had also been handed a heavy sentence for a Vancouver bank raid. The other two men were Harold Coullier and Claude Lavictoire, both charged with armed robberies.

When the four entered the yard they stayed together and made their way over to the west side of the enclosure. As they approached the yard's fence, they confronted a guard who was patrolling the roadway on the other side. One of the men pulled out an object, which the young and newly recruited officer believed to be a .38 calibre handgun, and pointed it directly at him. A second man yelled at the rookie, "Drop your gun!" Fearing for his life, he let his repeating rifle fall to the ground and stood motionless as the four prisoners hastily scrambled over the wire fence and dropped to the road in front of him. Wasylenchuk snatched up the rifle and the quartet ran up the hill towards the Gatehouse.

In the Gatehouse, a guard was reminiscing about prison life with Angus MacDonald, a former employee, who had just dropped off his brother-in-law for work. Suddenly the prisoners entered the building and one of them shouted, "This is a break." The Gatehouse guard showed great presence of mind and pressed the lever to drop the large front gate. This momentarily kept the escapees from leaving.

One of the inmates spotted a set of car keys in MacDonald's hand and demanded he turn them over. The civilian resisted and kicked the convict in the stomach. While the two scuffled, the others managed to open the Gatehouse door and ran up the narrow driveway. A guard was driving down it, on his way to work. The desperadoes dragged him out of his vehicle, and commandeered the car. They turned it around and began driving down the driveway towards Royal Oak Avenue. By this time MacDonald had run out to his car parked beside the Gatehouse and took off after the escapees. His 1950 Willys Station Wagon quickly gained on the offenders, and before they reached the end of the driveway, MacDonald slammed into the rear of their get-away car. As they collided, Wasylenchuk reached out the window with the rifle and fired two shots at MacDonald. One shot narrowly missed him and shattered the driver's side window, embedding broken glass into his scalp.

The force of the collision had caused the bumpers of the two vehicles to interlock, which compelled the fugitives to abandon the

All-to-often, police and the press converged at the Gatehouse.

car. MacDonald saw the men get out and come towards him. He locked the driver's side door, but it was to no avail. Wasylenchuk picked up the rifle and smashed the butt end through the door's window. Mac-Donald began to plead with the men that he had been shot and would co-operate with them. Upon seeing the blood run down his forehead, the felons must have believed him, for they simply dragged him out of the car and onto the pavement. They then went to work at trying to free the entangled cars. Wasylenchuk attempted to start MacDonald's station wagon but couldn't find the starter button, so he got out and ran.

In the frantic seconds that followed, several guards had run up to the melee and were trying to take the escapees back into custody. At the same time MacDonald noticed the rifle lying on the road. He grabbed the weapon and aimed it at Wasylenchuk as he ran down the driveway towards Royal Oak. He attempted to pull the trigger but the rifle was jammed and would not fire. He then took after the inmate on foot and chased him down the hill, but lost him as Wasylenchuk dove into the thick bush on the opposite side of Royal Oak Avenue.

All of the inmates had temporarily managed to free themselves from the guards in the lane and make it across the road, into the brambles. Within minutes police and guards had cordoned off the area and the manhunt began. After a few hours they flushed out Coullier and Lavictoire from a nearby field and returned them to the prison. By nightfall, 200 heavily-armed police and guards had failed to turn up any sign of the other two.

At 8:00 a.m. on Saturday, Warden Christie orchestrated a human chain of 100 men to line up twenty yards apart on Willingdon Avenue and begin a slow combing of the woods east towards Royal Oak Avenue. After two painstaking hours the men had made their way through the dense bog to Royal Oak with no signs of the fugitives.

Not until the early hours of Sunday morning was the first escapee, bald-headed Wasylenchuk, spotted only a few blocks south of the institution by the supervisor of the Young Offender's Unit. Police were dispatched to the scene and two RCMP officers, with their guns at the ready, closed in. Wasylenchuk was found hiding in a vacant parking lot underneath a pile of brambles. He gave up upon being surrounded. When arrested he was in good spirits, joking with the police and reporters, clean shaven, and wearing a woman's navy-blue coat. This led police to believe that he had a place of refuge for the night. Police also detained a man found within the block who was a known criminal and had a pocketful of U.S. and Mexican currency. Police believed this man was trying to meet up with Wasylenchuk to whisk him out of the country.

At the police station, Wasylenchuk told reporters that he had spent the first night under a woodpile near a collapsed chicken house on the property directly across from the prison. He said that guards and the police dog "Rip" had all passed within several feet of him more than once. The prisoner claimed that if he could have found a fedora to cover his bald head no one would have noticed him, and he would still be on the loose.

Only four hours after Wasylenchuk's arrest, police were advised by a 63-year-old machinist that he had been menaced by a man matching Lewis' description while working in his garage. He stated that he surprised a man when he walked into the garage and found him attempting to "hot wire" his vehicle. The suspect then grabbed a grease gun and told him to step inside a room. The machinist knocked the grease gun out of his hand and slammed a door in his face. He then chased him down a lane until he lost sight of him. Police swarmed the area, but again could not turn up any sign of the fugitive.

Several hours later, a man who was very grubby and seemed to be wearing a prison cap, took a taxi ride downtown. When the driver asked for the fare the man said that he had no cash, but offered his watch instead. The driver was suspicious; he later phoned the police and led them to where he had driven Lewis. When cornered, Lewis meekly surrendered and was returned to the prison.

This escape and manhunt attracted enormous publicity. It also instigated calls from Burnaby residents, especially those living beside the prison, to relocate the gaol and keep dangerous offenders in a more secure environment away from the city. This was the beginning of nearly forty years of lobbying by local residents for the closure of Oakalla.

For the Warden, things just went from bad to worse. The rehabilitation programs were in full swing, but to the outside world they were hardly noticed. Only the prison's troubles caught anyone's attention. In 1956 he had to face the toughest crisis of his career.

Loveless Taken Hostage
On December 19, 1955, 35-year-old Robert Tremblay, known in the criminal underworld as the "Frenchman," along with his associates Marcel Frenette, Charles Talbot, Lucien Mayers, and James Malgren, were found guilty of attempted murder and sentenced to twenty years in the penitentiary. Several months earlier, Robert Gordon had led Thomas Kinna, a self-confessed drug addict, down a trail to the False Creek Flats in Vancouver. At the bottom of the path, Tremblay and his gang ambushed Kinna, viciously beat him, and left him for dead. During the trial, much of the Crown's evidence relied on the testimony of Gordon. It was reported, however, that a deal had been worked out between Gordon and Tremblay's associates, and Gordon would recant on his evidence. Some time after this alleged agreement, Gordon was convicted of an unrelated theft charge and was about to be sent to jail. The

Vancouver Sun reported that Gordon made the following change of plans:

> Gordon decided to switch his Crown evidence because he learned through the criminal underground that he would be in danger or perhaps killed if he were sent to Oakalla. He then asked the magistrate to send him to any other jail than Oakalla. The attorney-general's office obtained an order-in-council committing him to the Nelson Gaol.
>
> Gordon knew he would be safe from any retaliation in the interior gaol and then, reportedly, he decided to go back on his promise to Tremblay's friends and "keep his mouth shut." [18]

The morning of May 7, 1956, was the final day of summations for the judges in the appeal of the five convicted men. Gordon had not recanted his evidence and Tremblay was furious. Frenette appeared in the B.C. Court of Appeal that morning to hear the decision. When the judges ruled to uphold the conviction, Frenette went wild and started yelling that they had been "framed" and "double crossed." He began demanding a new trial. The prisoner had to be restrained by two police officers and ushered out of the courtroom.

Frenette was returned to Oakalla while the West Wing was having their afternoon yard program. Once admitted, Frenette went straight out to the yard where he met with Tremblay and Talbot and informed them of the upheld conviction. Tremblay refused to accept his fate, and it was at this point that he began to mastermind a deadly plot to take a hostage.

The stairs leading to the West Wing yard were on the right side of the second landing of the Unit. Also on the this side of the landing, at the end of a long narrow corridor of cells, was the Wing's barber shop. In the shop were two pairs of long-handled straight-edged razors, a pair of scissors, and an electric barber's shears. Although the straight-edged razor was somewhat outdated and appeared more menacing than the newer disposable blade razors, the Warden defended its use:

> In the prison barber shop, a straight razor can be seen and checked constantly. If one disappears, it cannot be hidden easily by a prisoner. But a safety blade is another matter. They are the bane of institutions. They are small, but deadly, and can be hidden in the sole of

a shoe, slipped under a layer of paint, hidden in a million and one cracks and crannies. It must be remembered... that each one can kill you, but we have better control over the straight razors.[19]

At approximately 1:40 p.m., Tremblay, Frenette, and Talbot walked up the stairs from the exercise yard and onto the second landing. There they passed by Officer Jack Allinson, 25, who was supervising the yard, and senior guard Ernie Loveless, 38, who was sitting at a desk supervising telephone calls. The inmates told the two officers that they were going to get a hair cut and shave and continued to proceed down tier 2-Right towards the barber shop. At the end of the tier they found several inmates standing about so Tremblay told them to "get lost" because big things were about to happen. The trio then picked up the two straight razors and the pair of shears and headed back down the tier towards the endgate. As they approached the entrance to the landing, two of the prisoners rushed towards Loveless and the other lunged at Allinson. Loveless was quickly encircled by the pair and taken hostage. One prisoner held the razor to his throat, while the other pressed the cold tip of the scissors against his spine. Allinson tried to assist his partner but the third prisoner had the other razor held out towards his throat.

"Another step and you've had it," the inmate yelled. "Okay, Okay," replied Allinson, as he backed away. The inmate then told Allinson to get to the phone. As he was about to pick up the receiver, the phone rang. "Pick it up," he demanded. On the other end of the line was the records office inquiring about one of the unit's inmates. "Switch me to the Warden," said Allinson. The officer on the other end was confused and stated that he could not transfer the call. The hostage, shaking with anxiety, stammered, "Get me the Warden, quick!" He then hung up the telephone.

Christie was in his office talking to a social worker when the phone rang. "You're wanted in the West Wing," said the voice on the other end. Christie could hear the urgency in the man's voice and he immediately left for the Wing.

The trio had taken Loveless to the barber shop and ordered the remaining prisoners out. They bound his hands behind his back and tied his ankles together with an electric cord torn from the clippers. The officer was then seated in the barber's chair, with Frenette standing behind him holding the blade of the razor to his throat. By this time the Warden and several other staff members had arrived at the endgate. Tremblay began to scream obscenities at Christie. "Stay back — we have nothing to lose through cutting his throat," Tremblay yelled. "I've got life — what the hell... I'll cut his throat and roll his head out."[20]

Christie knew that Tremblay was desperate enough to carry out his threat. With the task of sparing an officer's life burning in his mind, the Warden attempted to negotiate. When he called upon Tremblay to explain his demands, the prisoner made no sense. He began to babble on about Gordon perjuring himself and that he should be given a new trial.

The Warden called Larry Hill, defence lawyer for the trio, to come to the prison right away to talk to the men. He also called for the best marksmen in the prison to go out to the rifle range and sight in their high-powered weapons. A short time later, two riflemen entered the West Wing and took up positions on the second landing. They then attempted to obtain an unobstructed view of the convicts through the maze of bars and wires. The men were ordered to shoot to kill the moment Christie gave the word.

The Warden then contacted Dr. Richmond, the prison physician, and had him prepare for an emergency. A surgeon was called in from Royal Columbian Hospital, and a large quantity of blood plasma was brought to the prison in a police car.[21]

Hill arrived at the prison shortly after 3:00 p.m. and agreed to speak with the inmates. He was sent down the narrow tier on his own, and by the time he reached his clients, Tremblay had changed his mind. He stated that he would now rather talk to a newspaper reporter than his lawyer, so that their story would be made public. Tremblay specified that he would see Bruce Larsen, City Editor of *The Province*. When the lawyer told this to Christie, he told the convicts that he had no way of forcing the newspaper editor to attend the prison, but agreed to try. Upon receiving the phone call, Larsen rushed to Oakalla and was on grounds by 3:15 p.m.

The scene upon his arrival was incredibly tense. Frenette had continued to keep the razor pressed to Loveless' throat for an hour and a half straight. The guard had now been moved from the barber's chair to lie face down on a mattress in the middle of the floor. The nerve-damaging wire cord around his wrists had been removed and replaced with a pair of handcuffs. The officer had remained silent the entire time except for at one point he yelled to the staff that he did not want his wife and family to know about the hostage-taking until it was "absolutely necessary." Tremblay was pacing back and forth in the room trying to bargain with the authorities, but he refused to talk to them face to face. He issued his demands to Talbot, who was kept busy running up and down the tier, taking messages between the prison officials at the endgate and the hostage-takers at the other end. Larsen believed that he had been called upon by Tremblay because the two had met the previous year when he went to the inmate's residence to collect a ninety-five dollar payment for a newspaper photographer's camera that Tremblay had damaged when he lashed out at the cameraman following a court appearance.

The Warden also contacted Tremblay's wife, to have her come to Oakalla to attempt to dissuade her husband from continuing this desperate act. Mrs. Tremblay was admitted into the West Wing at approximately 4:15 p.m. and was allowed to proceed onto the corridor with Hill. At the barber shop, Tremblay told his wife why he had done it and that he wouldn't give this up for anyone. He then told her to get out, which she did.

At 4:30 p.m. the three inmates demanded their dinner, and a few minutes later they had meal trays brought to them. Loveless was also sent a meal and they allowed him to eat. Christie and Dr. Richmond considered the possibility that they could end the ordeal by doping the food, but decided that drugs would take too long to take effect and it would just be too risky.

At about 6:00 p.m., on the direction of the Warden, Larsen began to talk to Talbot on how he could help resolve this crisis. Talbot told him that Tremblay wanted him to take down the true story of their attempted murder case. He demanded that their version be published, "Every word of it." Larsen stated that, within reason, he would do what he could. Tremblay was skeptical of the editor's response and wanted to be guaranteed that his story would be published. The felon stated he would not release his prisoner until his wife brought him in a newspaper that she bought from a news stand, so he could read it for himself. Larsen argued that this would take at least one whole day. Tremblay was adamant about seeing the story in print before releasing the hostage. For a short time the two men were at a stalemate. Meanwhile, the Warden was trying other routes to end the siege. One idea — to call in a priest (all three men stated they were Catholic) — proved futile. He kept coming back to the realization that he might have to trust in the accurate shooting of his marksmen.

Through his messenger, Talbot, Tremblay put forward another request: If the newspapers could put the story out that evening, he would let Loveless go. Larsen placed a call to his superior to see what could be done. Within minutes they received confirmation that the paper could print an "extra" edition. Crews would be called into work to start up the printing machines, and the extra edition would be on the streets in a matter of hours.

At the same time, Tremblay told Larsen that most of their story could be obtained from interviewing inmates Talbot, Malgren, and his lawyer Hill. After which, he stated, he would talk to Larsen personally. Malgren was brought into an interview room from another tier in the wing and questioned by the editor. Meanwhile, Tremblay was sent a pencil and paper to write out his side of the agreement. As he sat down and started to write, he suddenly let out a yell and threw his hands in the air. For a moment everyone tensed until Tremblay sat down and started writing again.

When he was finished, Tremblay passed the paper out to Christie, and on it he had stated several additional demands. He wanted this affair kept within the province, and demanded that the Attorney-General study the case and decide if it warranted court reconsideration. Although his patience was wearing thin, Christie telephoned Victoria and spoke to the Deputy Attorney-General, who agreed to review the case. By this time, Larsen had finished interviewing the others. He and Hill then walked alone to the barber shop to hear Tremblay's story. Larsen later recalled:

> I stood in the door of the room, Tremblay slid a stool to me, but I continued standing. Lawyer Hill sat on an inverted washtub, Frenette stood over Loveless, who was hidden from our view behind blanketing and a barber chair. Tremblay's opening remark: "Don't be scared Bruce... come in." I asked him to describe his complaint... Tremblay sat smoking as I wrote it down.... After twenty minutes I told him I had sufficient to combine with what I got from Malgren. I said: "Now why don't you let Loveless walk out of here with me?" [22]

Tremblay had relaxed somewhat, but he still wasn't completely satisfied that the story would be printed. He didn't want to take the chance of releasing the hostage without publicity for his cause. Larsen began to plead with Tremblay: "I'll admit we've got a story and you should know we'll be running it. I assure you of that. Our paper's called out crews — we'll be publishing." [23] The three inmates started to waver and huddled to discuss the proposal. After a few minutes Talbot returned and wanted the issue of reprisals addressed. The inmates wanted to know if they would have to do a lot of time in solitary and would other privileges be lost. Christie said that, unless he was ordered otherwise, they would not go to isolation and, for the

Guard Ernie Loveless (left) and *Province* editor Bruce Larsen share a light moment following their hostage ordeal.

time being, they would have exercise periods at different times than the others.

With that statement, Tremblay's attitude changed dramatically. Everyone could feel the tension subsiding. The prisoners had another short meeting, and then Tremblay decided to surrender. Frenette released Loveless, who got up off the floor, walked on rubbery legs over to Larsen, and thanked him. Then Hill, Larsen, and Loveless walked off the tier with the three felons following close behind. The siege had lasted until 7:25 p.m. For Ernie Loveless, that meant that for more than five hours his life was balanced on a razor's edge. That night, only a few hours after the drama had ended, an extra edition of *The Province* hit the streets. The banner headline read: "THIS STORY FOR A LIFE!"

On November 23, 1956, Tremblay and Frenette received additional one-year terms for their part in the hostage-taking. The Crown entered a stay of proceedings against Talbot, who had acted as a messenger. The inmates had pleaded not guilty, by reason of insanity. Despite his traumatic experience, Ernie Loveless continued to serve as an Oakalla guard, eventually achieving an upper-management position.

Graham's Gift

Robert Graham, 23, was a tough member of a Vancouver gang. In late 1955 he kicked a man to death in a gas station parking lot while his gang held the victim's friends back from coming to his aid. In December Graham was sentenced to death. While waiting on Death Row, he was seen by ministers and other religious visitors. Only three weeks before he was to die he became a Christian and his personality changed profoundly. Instead of wanting to hurt people, he now wanted to help them. Knowing that there was little he could do to repay society for his crimes in the time left to him, Graham decided that he would help society in his death. He would donate his eyes to the blind upon his execution. Just days before his death he completed the necessary donor paperwork.

At midnight on May 22, 1956, Graham stepped onto the grey trap doors and joined the minister in a prayer. There was a slight smile on his lips as the hood was placed over his head. As the minister finished the prayer the lever to the doors was released. After the hanging, his body was taken to Vancouver General Hospital where doctors removed the corneas from his eyes. Within twelve hours of his death, Graham's corneas were successfully transplanted onto the eyes of a blind eight-year-old boy.

Police Slayer Hanged

Early in the afternoon of December 7, 1955, Joe Gordon and James Carey set out to rob a bank in south-east Vancouver. They were armed with a .38 calibre revolver and a .45 calibre automatic, respectively. By the time the men arrived at the bank it had closed for the day. Gordon was frustrated as he desperately needed some quick money to pay for, among other things, outstanding lawyer's fees. The two men decided that they would go on a spree of robbing small businesses in order to raise some cash. Carey returned to his home and picked up his common-law wife, Noreen, and their baby — as he had promised her a drive. They then met up with a male acquaintance, who would drive the get-away car. After deciding against robbing an office on Commercial Drive, the four drove over to a lot underneath the Granville Street Bridge, where they staked out another business.

Shortly after 7:00 p.m. Vancouver City Constable Gordon Sinclair was working a one-man patrol in Kitsilano when he and another two-man patrol unit were dispatched to investigate a citizen report of two suspicious-looking men hanging around the Watkins-Winram plant at Third and Granville. Sinclair was first on the scene when he spotted the men. As he pulled his car up to the curb on the left side of the street, the two men ran away. Sinclair called out to them to stop; Carey kept running, but Gordon stopped and walked back toward the patrol car. As he neared the police vehicle, Officer Sinclair opened his car door and began to get out. Gordon drew his handgun, pointed it at Sinclair, and shot him in the face at point-blank range. The .38 calibre bullet pierced the left side of the officer's cheek and exited on the right side of his head. As the officer fell dead to the pavement, the slayer shot him again in the back. Gordon ran around to the rear of the building to where Carey was waiting for him, they jumped into a dark blue convertible and roared away.

As the other responding unit approached the scene, the officers spotted Gordon as he ran across the parking lot and into the car. Unaware of their fellow officer's fate, the police chased the vehicle until it slowed down a few blocks later and the two suspects bailed out. One constable chased the suspects on foot, but lost them as they ran through an apartment complex. The other continued after the driver of the get-away car, but lost sight of it as it sped east along Fir Street. The officers then returned to the plant, where they discovered the veteran officer lying face down in the street. Officer Sinclair was pronounced "dead on arrival" at Vancouver General Hospital.

Reaction to the murder was swift. A massive man-hunt, by all on-duty and many off-duty members who had heard of the tragedy, was mounted, with roadblocks set up around the city. An intensive search of the area around the crime scene turned up the .45 calibre handgun and a mask. Numerous cars matching the description of the suspect vehicle were checked without success. Then an officer remembered that a convict he knew owned a dark-blue 1953 Ford convertible. When police confronted the man, he told them that he had lent his car to a friend, although he would not reveal who. Acting on a hunch, officers moved in on an apartment flat, rented by a person who associated with the owner of the car, where they arrested four men and a 19-year-old woman, and held them in gaol pending their investigation. One of the men held was 33-year-old "salesman" Joe Gordon, a well-known Vancouver area armed robber. He had been released on $15,000 bail only days earlier, and was to appear in court on the day following the shooting, accused of robbing a Bank of Commerce of $26,000 on November 26. Carey was not arrested at the time as he had fled to eastern Canada. Police did not have enough evidence to sustain a murder charge, and released Gordon and the others.

Police got their second break in the case just over a week later, when an informant led police to the location of a .38 calibre revolver hidden in the garden of a home on West 10th Avenue. The handgun turned out to be the murder weapon. Gordon was connected to the gun and he was re-arrested on weapons offences. Around the same time, police were able to confirm that Noreen Carey had been an occupant of the get-away car. She was interrogated by the police and provided a written statement incriminating Gordon. While in custody at Oakalla, Gordon was informed that he was also being charged with the murder of Constable Sinclair.

After Gordon's preliminary hearing, a material witness warrant for the arrest of James Carey was issued. He was arrested in Toronto on February 15. Back in Vancouver, Carey provided police with a full written statement fingering Gordon as the murderer of the constable. Carey was subsequently charged with the murder of the officer as well. On April 26, 1956, after fourteen days of trial, both men were convicted of the murder of Officer Sinclair; much of the Crown's evidence had relied on Carey's statement. The pair were sentenced to hang on April 2, 1957.

Joe Gordon considered himself a poet of sorts, and while in Oakalla he wrote numerous poems and letters. In the final days before his execution, the gaol-house poet wrote letters to his lawyer, rabbi, and fellow prisoners. He also wrote a warning to parents to guard their children against delinquency, which was printed in the *Vancouver Sun* on the day of his death. This was not, however, Gordon's final message. On the night before his hanging, he penned one last note in which he expressed his spite for James Carey. He wrote: "I have yet to meet a stool pigeon who would not sell his miserable soul for a phony three-dollar bill. This case proves that."[24] Gordon was referring to the fact that Carey's incriminating statements likely saved his own neck. Only fourteen hours before he was scheduled to die, Carey's sentence was commuted to life imprisonment. He had argued that he was only with Gordon on the night of the slaying to spy on him for the RCMP.

Although the Warden delayed the execution of Gordon for five minutes, to allow for a last-minute reprieve by Ottawa, Gordon paid the price for the cold-blooded murder of a police officer shortly after midnight on April 2, 1957.

Oakalla's Final Execution

Leo Anthony Mantha had the unfortunate distinction of being the last man hanged at Oakalla. In September 1958 the 33-year-old sailor was involved in a homosexual relationship with 23-year-old Aaron Jenkins. One night the two got into a violent fight when Jenkins told Mantha that he wanted to end their relationship and marry his girlfriend. Later that night, as Jenkins was sleeping in his quarters aboard the *HMCS Naden,* Mantha crept down to his bed, drew a knife, and repeatedly stabbed him in the throat.

Mantha was convicted of the murder in December that year; however, his lawyer hoped that his death sentence would be commuted to a life sentence. Only days before Mantha was scheduled to hang, another Oakalla prisoner on Death Row had his death sentence commuted. He had been slated to die alongside Mantha, for murdering his brother during a family argument. In addition, a telegram had been sent to the Federal Department of Justice pleading for a reprieve. In recent years there had been a surge of opposition to capital punishment, and debates over hanging had become more frequent. Several Members of Parliament had recently witnessed executions and some found them "barbarous." For Mantha, the government replied to the request by stating that it would not interfere with the course of justice. Shortly after midnight on April 28, 1959, Leo Mantha was executed.

Mantha was not the last person in Oakalla to sit on Death Row. Other men convicted of murderous crimes waited on the lonely tier, wondering if their lives would soon come to the same violent end as their victims'. For some of them it was a close call; however, all of their sentences were eventually commuted. Capital punishment was finally abolished from the Criminal Code in 1976, long after Hugh Christie was gone.

Citizen Captures Fleeing Felons

Escapees were not always free once they cleared the barbed-wire fences. On several occasions citizens became directly involved in the recapture of felons on the run. On July 31, 1962 two of five prisoners learned this lesson the hard way.

The gaolbreak began with a dangerous inmate, Murray Boyd, 24, who was being held in the underground Segregation Unit for breaking the Rules and Regulations in the Main Gaol. It was during Boyd's one-hour ablution period that the trouble started. He was out of his cell, permitted to take a shower and exercise on the open tier, when one of the two guards in the unit left the area to get some clean towels. When the second guard was alone, Boyd lunged at him with a knife and took him hostage by pressing the home-made shiv into his abdomen. He then threatened to kill him if he did not follow his demands. Boyd ordered the officer to open one of the cell doors, pushed the guard into the cell, and locked the gate behind him.

He then waited for the second officer to return with his armful of towels. When the guard entered the corridor, Boyd jumped him and held the knife to his back. He brought the guard in front of the cell holding the first officer, and yelled at him to throw out his keys or he would kill the man he held. The officer quickly produced the Segregation Unit keys and handed them over to the convict.

Boyd then hurriedly unlocked four cells holding other unmanageable offenders. Within seconds, they were out the front door and looking around the property for a means of escape. Locating a parked garbage truck a short distance away, they "hot-wired" it and drove quietly across the prison grounds and up to the Gatehouse entrance. There they were waved through the front gates by unsuspecting staff. It was only after the truck had passed through the gate, that a guard spotted the prisoners inside and sounded the alarm.

Once outside the prison property, the escapees abandoned the vehicle and split into two groups. Three of the men, including Boyd, ran south towards Kingsway, while the other two ran north. At the 3800 block of Kingsway, Alex MacKay, 32, a local fireman and former athletic star, was sitting in his car minding his own business. He knew that trouble was up when three desperate-looking men, dressed in prison garb, came running towards his car. As they approached, he jumped out and confronted them. One of the fugitives attacked, and the fight was on. Another managed to get into the car and start the ignition, but MacKay reached in through the window, grabbed the keys, and threw them as far as he could. As fists continued to fly, Mackay's superior strength began to take its toll. The bloodied and bruised felons tried to make a run for it. MacKay chased them, caught up with one of them and was able to hold him until police arrived. Boyd and the other prisoner got away, but Boyd's partner was captured in the area within an hour. The other two fugitives, who had run

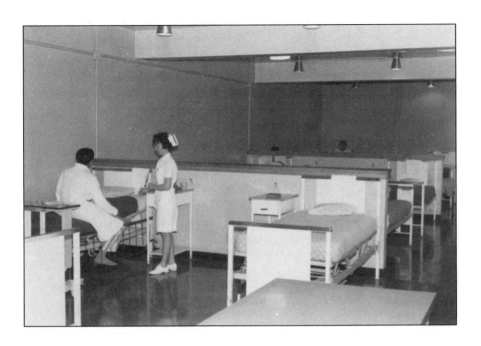

Nursing ward, Health Care Centre.

towards Deer Lake, were apprehended several days later by Boston Bar RCMP who found them sleeping on a train near Lytton. Boyd himself was not recaptured for some time.

Overcrowding Protested

The final crisis to face Hugh Christie was a disturbance staged on September 22, 1962. Prisoners in the West Wing refused to return to their cells after an exercise period and protested about "overcrowding, poor quality of food, and inadequate laundry and shower facilities."[25] Extra staff were called in, but the situation did not further escalate and, after a short time, all of the inmates agreed to return to their cells. There was no doubt that conditions were deplorable as the prison population reached an all-time high. Even prisoners housed in the Old Gaol had to be double-bunked, while more than forty others were placed in makeshift cells in the basement of the gymnasium. By the following year, the count had peaked 1200, and eight portable trailers had to be brought onto the farm to provide living quarters for ninety inmates. The dorms were used for those employed in the piggery, barns, and garbage disposal. Apart from relieving overcrowding, the trailers kept the odorous inmates away from the rest of the population.

One of the final achievements Christie was able to observe during his last years as warden was the opening of the new Health Care Centre. In early 1962, the majority of young offenders were transferred from Oakalla to the Haney Correctional Centre, and in October, the old Young Offender's Unit re-opened as the new hospital. The centre had the capacity to segregate prisoners with infectious diseases, and its facilities included a laboratory, x-ray room, pharmacy, dental office, and an operating theater. This meant fewer prisoners would have to be escorted to local hospitals for treatment, thereby reducing the potential for escapes. In the years that followed, the Health Care Centre became the central medical facility for all correctional centres in British Columbia. It was one of the final progressive changes implemented at Oakalla in the name of "rehabilitation."

Six

Warehousing Prisoners
1963-1974

After a decade of service, Hugh Christie resigned and moved to Ottawa to join the External Affairs Department. His successor was Warren Harding Mulligan, 42, former warden of the Prince George Gaol. Originally from Saskatchewan, Mulligan moved to Langley in 1934, and shortly afterwards enlisted in the Royal Canadian Navy. He served for seven years before retiring to find a new career with the Corrections Branch. Hired as an Oakalla guard in 1949, he transferred to Prince George six years later to become the deputy warden. Within a year he was warden.

By the 1960s, the fifty-year-old gaol was showing signs of deterioration. The staff were aware that sharp objects could easily chisel away the crumbling mortar and bricks, and there was a real threat of escapes through the walls of the Main Gaol. No one, however, considered the possibility of inmates escaping directly from within their cells. The columns of cells were in the centre of each unit, and there was no direct access to the outside walls. Inmates would first have to free themselves from their cells, then escape from the tiers, and finally breach the brick walls before being clear of the Main Gaol.

In 1963, two felons acted upon this false sense of security.

On August 13, inmates Barber and Crnec were housed together in the second cell on the left side of the top floor in the West Wing. Earlier, they had obtained a screwdriver and by the end of the day they had almost chiselled a hole through the ceiling of their cell. They were left relatively free to work between 3:00 p.m. and 11:00 p.m. because there were only four guards on-duty, who were preoccupied supervising inmate phone calls, watching prisoners on the lower exercise tier, and other duties. The prisoners also had the perfect location to conduct their escape. From their cell they had a clear view of officers climbing the stairs on the left side of the unit, and a window a short distance away provided a reflection of guards approaching from the other side. Thus they were able to stop chiselling and camouflage the hole before the officers were within earshot.

The inmates were seen in their cell at 11:00 p.m. when the guards cleared a head-count of all prisoners for the oncoming graveyard shift. At 3:15 a.m., an officer making his rounds noticed that a hole, two foot wide, had been burrowed through four-and-a-half inches of concrete leading from the ceiling of the cell to the roof of the West Wing. As the officer gazed through the hole into the starlit night, the escapees had already made their way off the roof and were well beyond the surrounding fence. Upon hearing of the escape, the new warden also went through the roof. He ordered an extra four inches of concrete to be laid on top of the entire Main Gaol. This incident, however, was only a minor set-back. The first true test of Mulligan's leadership came on his first anniversary as warden.

West Wing Riot

Tension began to mount in the remand West Wing early in 1964. As in the previous riot, the prisoners involved were awaiting either trial or transfer to the penitentiary. Many of the prison's chronic problems, such as overcrowding, were still present more than a decade later. However, two major issues were identified as contributing factors in this new build-up of hostilities.

The first, and most stressful, was the newly implemented *Habitual Criminal Act* initiated by the federal government. The conditions of the Act allowed the Crown to ask for indefinite sentences for individuals who had persistently been involved in criminal activity. That is, if a person had been convicted of three or more charges in which he or she was liable to imprisonment for more than five years, the Crown could proceed to have him or her labelled a "habitual criminal;" which theoretically meant a life sentence. In 1964, there were at least a dozen men in Oakalla who had been notified that these proceedings were being initiated against them.

The second major problem was the high number of heroin and other drug addicts. The true addicts suffered from severe withdrawal while in prison and required constant medical supervision. Medical staff would administer sedatives, usually mild narcotics, to counteract the effects. Other convicts, who were not addicts, faked addiction so that they could receive drugs. This posed a dilemma for the medical personnel, who were required to prescribe medication for addicts, but to refuse drugs to inmates who appeared to be feigning addiction. With approximately thirty frustrated drug addicts in the West Wing and a dozen inmates facing prosecution under the *Habitual Criminal Act,* in May 1964, the stage was set for a major disturbance.

At approximately 10:00 p.m. on May 8, newly admitted inmate R. Brunelle underwent a routine medical examination. He told Dr. Turpin, the examining Medical Officer, that he was a drug addict and required withdrawal medication. The doctor thoroughly examined Brunelle and concluded that he would suffer no withdrawal effects while in prison. After prescribing a mild sedative (three grains of Tuinal), he sent Brunelle back to his unit.

When he returned to the West Wing to be locked up for the night, he told his fellow prisoners that he had been refused withdrawal medication. Inmate T. Irvine who was very unruly and suffered from psychiatric disorders, called out to staff that Brunelle had not been properly treated and demanded that he be given his drugs. The Principal Officer in the wing checked with the doctor, who assured him that Brunelle was not a drug addict and did not require treatment. A guard went to Irvine's cell and explained this to him, and he agreed to settle down.

As soon as the lights were turned out and the radio system shut off, Irvine once again began to call out and started banging his cup on the cell bars. Others joined in the clamour and they threatened to "smash up" their cells. At this point the Principal Officer contacted the Night Gaoler and told him that, if Irvine was not removed to the Isolation Unit, a disturbance might erupt. He agreed, and extra staff were called in from the East Wing to remove him. Three guards went to the prisoner's cell, opened the door, and ordered him to come out. He refused and told the officers to leave him alone or they would get "lumped." Officer D. Olson went into the cell first, and as he did, Irvine punched him in the face. The guard returned the punch and the fight was on. The convict resisted violently and continuously as he was dragged out of his cell and off the tier. One of the officers used a neck restraint head-lock, so that the other guards could handcuff him. Many of the other prisoners who observed this claimed that staff had used excessive force and they became even more enraged.

Once he was removed to "the hole" the rest of the prisoners became restless. They banged their cell bars and threatened to destroy the Unit if Irvine was not returned to his cell. The Principal Officer had no wish to see a riot ignite, but, at the same time, he did not want inmates to consider him weak by acceding to their demand. He once again consulted with the Night Gaoler. At that moment one of the prisoners on the third tier smashed the toilet in his cell. As they spoke over the telephone, they could overhear the cheers of inmates as the fixtures were being smashed. The senior officer gave the order to have the inmate returned to his cell before any more property was damaged. Once Irvine was returned, the Unit quietened down and there were no further incidents throughout the night.

The next morning, May 9, 1964, was fairly quiet, and following breakfast, the usual clean up of the Unit began. Security Officer J. Simpson was in charge of supervising the third tier on the left side when inmate Austin Tarleck approached him. He stated that his nerves were real edgy and the ruckus the night before had upset him. He was also concerned about being charged as a habitual criminal. Tarleck had a history of twenty-seven convictions, dating back to 1930, for armed robbery, drugs, and other serious offences. Simpson passed this information on to his supervisor, who told him that he had known Tarleck for a long time and that he was, "a perpetual complainer — he always seems to be whining about something — always wants something."[1] At about 11:00 a.m., Simpson observed Tarleck in his cell crying, and also reported this to his supervisor. When he did not come out of his cell for lunch, the Principal Officer contacted the hospital and asked if they would pay the prisoner a visit. The medical staff stated that his file would be reviewed and that he would be seen sometime after lunch.

Shortly after noon an inmate approached a guard and reported that there was a prisoner hanging in a cell on 3-left. Several officers ran to the third tier and made their way down the left side. In cell 17 they found Tarleck hanging by strips of bedding. His body was lowered to the floor and Security Officer J. Gardiner immediately began to apply mouth-to-mouth resuscitation and then heart massage. Within minutes an inhalator crew, ambulance, and doctor had arrived, but they were unable to revive him. Tarleck was pronounced dead at 12:30 p.m.

For the next few hours the Wing remained relatively peaceful and the regular exercise yard program went ahead as planned. When the

Idle prisoners confined to the narrow tiers of the Main Gaol.

men in the yard were called to return to the Wing, they refused. The Warden was contacted at home and advised of the suicide and sit-in. When he arrived, he informed the prisoners that he would meet with representatives only if they returned to their cells. After pondering their next move for two hours, the men agreed to leave the yard. The Warden met with three inmates who made several general complaints and two specific ones. First, they felt that Irvine had been removed from his cell without any justification and the officers had used excessive force against him. Second, they believed Tarleck should have received greater medical attention, and they wanted to be assured that anyone who wanted treatment would be given it immediately. The Warden told the men that he would look into the whole situation and get back to them in two weeks. He asked them to be civil in the meantime and set examples to the others.

An uneasy calm settled on the West Wing, but it only lasted until just after night lock-up. At 11:00 p.m., Brunelle called out again for withdrawal medication. He was taken to the hospital and examined by Dr. Turpin, who again told him that he did not require further medication and sent him away. When Mulligan was advised, he suggested to Turpin that, because of the explosive situation in the West Wing, Brunelle be given a strong dose of medicine. The doctor sent the medication over to the administration area and Brunelle was sent there to take it. He took the drug and returned to the cellblock. When he was locked in his cell he told the others that once again he got "bugger all."

There was little noise in the Wing for another full hour, but shortly after 1:00 a.m., just as the prisoners watched the afternoon shift get into their cars and leave the parking lot, bedlam broke loose. At that time, there were only three officers and the Warden on duty for the whole gaol. Until reinforcements arrived an hour later, they were on their own — and it was during this time that most of the damage occurred. The inmates smashed windows, lights, and the contents of their cells. All the four officers could do was fight fires from the safety of the landings. When eleven extra staff arrived, the West Wing was in complete darkness and filled with smoke and water. Emergency lighting was produced and the staff soon had a handle on the situation. In Warden Mulligan's report, he indicated the difficult task the officers faced that night:

> During the long night of continuous noise, breaking and rebreaking of porcelain fixtures, firing of bedding and clothing, and breaking of lights, the fifteen staff members on duty in the West Wing Unit conducted themselves admirably. I have commended them for their impeccable conduct and efficiency under the trying and dangerous circumstances. While it was often dangerous for staff to patrol in front of the cells, because of flying porcelain, etc., after the incident of attempted suicides by Turner and Sanford at about 1:45

a.m., and the discovery that inmates in cells 5 left 14 and 5 left 15 were chopping their way through the concrete wall between the cells under the cover of continuous noise, it was felt necessary to keep staff patrolling all tiers constantly. The staff carried out my directions in this respect without flinching, dodging missiles and, thereby, preventing any further escape attempts. This turned out to be no easy task when it is considered that officers had to move, for the most part, with emergency lights, walking over piles of debris and wading through water from burst plumbing lines and fire hoses.[2]

On the morning of May 10, there were no further acts of destruction, but many threatened to "slash" themselves with pieces of glass or porcelain. Inmate Irvine tried to hang himself, and would have succeeded if not for the efforts of Officer Gardiner, who revived him. There were also very few injuries to both staff and prisoners throughout the ruckus. The only serious injury occurred when an inmate severely cut his left leg while kicking his toilet bowl to pieces.

The total damage became apparent in the morning when staff surveyed the West Wing. The toilets and/or sinks in fifty-four of the cells were completely destroyed. Numerous beds, side tables, and countless windows were also ruined. The total cost of the uproar was in excess of $30,000. In the aftermath, thirty-two inmates were charged in Magistrate's Court with damaging public property, and twenty-nine received additional prison terms of up to eighteen months.

The riot had been futile. The Wing continued to be swamped with drug addicts, the *Habitual Criminal Act* proceeded, and living conditions were further strained as inmates had to be shifted around while the cells were repaired.

Suicide Crisis

The greatest concern for Warden Mulligan was the high number of suicides that occurred over a four-year period during the mid-1960s. It was a time of suicide "hysteria," when hundreds of inmates either attempted suicide, committed suicide, or viciously mutilated their own bodies.

Up until the 1950s suicides at Oakalla were relatively rare, and for the most part, were not made public. The first suicide to generate publicity was on July 8, 1953, when 39-year-old convicted murderer Walter Pavlukoff stabbed himself to death in the West Wing. Pavlukoff had previously been held in the South Wing on Death Row, with a twenty-four-hour guard. However, when he appealed his conviction he was allowed to be housed with the regular remand population until his appeal was settled. On the date of his suicide, he had just been brought back from court after learning that his appeal had been turned down. Although Pavlukoff told several officers that he had lost his appeal, the courts had not yet officially notified Oakalla, and he was allowed to return to his cell. Less than an hour later, a guard went to check on him and found him lying face down on the floor of his cell in a pool of blood. He had fashioned a small, yet razor-sharp, knife and stabbed himself in the chest. Pavlukoff had been scheduled to hang three weeks later.

Almost a year to the day later, there was another sensational suicide. Elmer Ranta was a 46-year-old vagrant who had a record of twenty-one terms of imprisonment at Oakalla which included several trips to Essondale Mental Institution. On July 2, 1954, he tried to take his life by hanging himself with shoelaces. Authorities had him moved to the prison hospital for observation. The only exercise facilities for these men was on the roof of the Administration Wing. On the morning of July 5, while Ranta was out for his one-hour exercise period, he scaled the fence surrounding the roof and lowered himself onto the narrow outside ledge. As he threatened to jump, the Warden ordered guards to fetch blankets, while another officer crawled out onto the ledge to plead with him. As a crowd gathered to watch the drama unfold, Ranta leaped from his perch and plunged fifty feet to his death, landing on the front steps of the institution. Following the tragedy, more barbed and razor-ribbon wire were placed around the yard to deter others.

There were actually only three suicides at Oakalla between 1953 and 1963. However, this decade saw a general deterioration in the overall mental health of Oakalla's inmates. In the 1964/65 annual report Dr. Richmond noted:

> There has been a marked increase in pathological behaviour within the gaol. This has taken the form of 5 suicides and 57 attempted suicides, of which 27 were slashing, 17 were attempted hangings, 10 were by swallowing metal (spoons etc.), 2 swallowing toxic substances, and 1 attempted drowning.

By early September 1966, the crisis had reached a point where some offenders were in a complete frenzy — two had committed suicide in a three-week period. On September 14, Mulligan, testifying at his fifth Coroner's Inquest that year, said: "The word [of a suicide] spreads through the prison and unstable prisoners become hysterical."[3] Two days later, the year's sixth suicide victim, 37-year-old Joseph Bernier, hanged himself with a bed sheet tied to his bunk in the West Wing. He had attempted to kill himself twice before and was awaiting habitual criminal proceedings at the time of his death. At the Coroner's Inquest, an RCMP Officer read a suicide note left by Bernier:

> I am sick to my stomach with all these suicides and slashings since I have been here. It is getting on my nerves. I have a record and now they want me in jail for life for crimes I have already paid for so I will give them what they want. I only hope the City Prosecutor Stewart McMorran, Magistrate James Bartman and all those detectives on the burglary squad sleep well now that I am dead....[4]

The suicide led to a public outcry for changes at Oakalla. In response, Attorney-General Robert Bonner announced that an inquiry would be conducted into these incidents to determine how surveillance of prisoners could be improved. The result of the inquiry was the establishment of a suicide prevention unit or "Observation Unit" on the top floor of the South Wing. The 12-cell facility allowed for almost constant monitoring of Oakalla's most violent, depressed, and suicidal men. The success of the new Observation Unit was not readily apparent; in 1966/67 there were six suicides. Dr. Richmond appealed for a new psychiatric facility, as the Observation Unit was continuously full.

Although the number of self-inflicted injuries continued to climb in 1968, successful suicides were reduced by half over the previous year. In August, the prison compiled statistics on all attempted and successful suicides during the previous four years. A total of 391 self-inflicted injuries were reported (including seventeen successful suicides) by 229 inmates (see Appendix C). Of all the successful suicides, seventy-seven percent were first attempts.

As the years passed, and the high remand population slowly dropped, so too did the number of attempted and successful suicides. Even with this reduction, the Warden and his staff were still heavily criticized by the press whenever one occurred. Mulligan felt that much of this was unwarranted:

> It seems that the mentally ill or temporarily disturbed person who is bound to take his own life will most

likely succeed in spite of staff vigilance. The only possible sure control over such potential tragedies would be either placing some individuals in constant restraint for lengthy periods or keeping them under the direct continuous observation of a single staff member. The first suggestion is too medieval to contemplate and the second, of course, is impossible with the large number of disturbed inmates who are admitted to and pass through the Centre.[5]

Unfortunately, no matter how vigilant Corrections Officers may have been, the fact remained that Oakalla held many desperate and emotionally disturbed persons, who saw suicide as the only way out of their painful situations.

"A Violent Struggle"

Correctional Officer T. Harris was a well-liked staff member. Not only did he get along well with other guards, but many of the convicts found him friendly and easy going. On occasion, he had even found some of them job placements.

At about eight in the morning of October 20, 1966, Harris escorted a gang of ten men from Westgate "A" to the gymnasium to do some clean-up work. Within half an hour, Harris staggered back to Westgate "A" Unit alone, semi-conscious, and covered from head to foot in his own blood.

When armed officers rushed to the gymnasium they found the front doors wide open and two of the ten prisoners missing. In Warden Mulligan's report he documented the gruesome sight the officers discovered:

> There was evidence of a violent struggle in the interior of the gym near the north entrance. Metal frame chairs were overturned and some were bent. Many chairs were spotted and smeared with blood. Bloody hand prints were in evidence on several places on the floor covering. In addition to many other spots and smears of blood on the floor there were also two large blood pools. Blood was smeared on the door frame and on the gate post of the outside fence. A paring knife was found on the gym floor and keys to the gymnasium were found on the stage.[6]

Officer Harris suffered a deep laceration on his scalp, both his right and left hands were badly fractured, he sustained five broken ribs, and a skull fracture. The majority of the wounds were defensive and it was believed that Harris would have been killed if he had given up the courage to fend off the blows of the bludgeoning chairs by using his hands and arms.

The two escapees, Clarke and McCann, made their way past the north end of the Warden's residence and over the west fence of the prison, where a plastic bag of clothes had been stashed for them. In Vancouver they met up with a friend who loaned them his car and supplied them with drugs. The pair then drove into the Fraser Valley, but as the drugs took effect and impaired their ability to drive, they were spotted by police and arrested in Matsqui. Both were later charged with, and received sentences for, prison break with violence and assaulting a peace officer.

A Lover's Quarrel
On Boxing Day, 1966, Dr. Richmond was involved in negotiating yet another violent incident. The East Wing drama began when two drug-addicted homosexual partners were about to be separated. One of them had been swearing at a staff member earlier that morning and was informed that he would be sent to the South Wing Observation Unit. He pleaded with the Officer In Charge not to be sent out of the Unit, and after some discussion, the guard allowed him to stay, if he behaved himself. Shortly after this, the same prisoner then attempted to visit his lover, who was cleaning an empty tier on the fifth landing. The supervising officer had to turn his attention away to confront the inmate who had come just come up the flight of stairs. As the guard reprimanded him for attempting to make the visit, the other prisoner crept off the landing and went down the set of stairs behind the guard's back.[7]

A few minutes later, both had managed to make their way to the Barber Shop on tier 2-Left. From there they were able to climb the screen surrounding the shop and gain access to the two cat-walks above them. They then proceeded to kick out the windows on the left side of the Unit. As staff and inmates ran from the shower of glass coming to the floor, one of the prisoners produced a twelve-inch knife, defying anyone to approach him, and threatening to kill the officers who were now watching from a safe distance. At that moment his partner wrenched an entire window frame from the wall and threw it to the floor. This triggered off the first inmate who picked up plates of glass and flung them like frisbees at the staff. As everyone scrambled for cover, they ran up and down the cat-walks pelting the

Unit with glass, ripping wooden planks from the floorboards, and smashing light fixtures. One of the prisoners then slashed his forearm with a piece of glass.

The Deputy Warden was called to the Wing. He sent for Dr. Richmond, who had counselled these two on numerous occasions. The physician first asked all staff members to leave the area so that he could talk to them in private, as he knew they both felt threatened by the guards. He also decided to appeal to their desire for drugs, and in an effort to peacefully end the crisis, he promised to give them a strong dose if they came down from the cat-walks. After some discussion they agreed and were taken to the Dispensary Office where they were given their promised narcotic. The pair were then taken into custody by the staff.

The incident did not end at this point. After they were treated, they were taken to the South Wing Observation Ward. Early the following morning, one of them got hold of a sharp instrument and re-slashed his arm. The prisoner was taken to the Dispensary but he refused treatment. To prevent him from further harming himself he was placed in restraints and taken to the Isolation Unit. Only fifteen minutes after the first inmate slashed his arm, the second slashed his arms and torso. He was taken to the prison hospital were Dr. Richmond required more than 100 sutures to close his wounds.

Crashing the Gates

Early in the morning of March 9, 1967, Vocational Instructor Uncles was supervising a prisoner on a sewing machine at one end of the Westgate Upholstery Shop when he was suddenly taken hostage by inmates David Bird, 18, Neil Turner, 23, and 17-year-old Brian West:

> Inmate Turner grabbed me from behind approximately around my face area and put a ten to twelve inch blade in my throat. He said,"O.K. down on your knees." I went down on my knees and Inmate West said,"down on your stomach." Turner grabbed one arm and West grabbed the other, securing with tieing twine behind my back and around my wrists. Then Turner said, "up on your feet and go to the front of the shop." I did not say one word at all. He said, "stand by the drill press." He then turned the drill press on and told me to stand beside it, all the time holding the knife at my back. Inmate Turner then went to the grindstone and Inmate

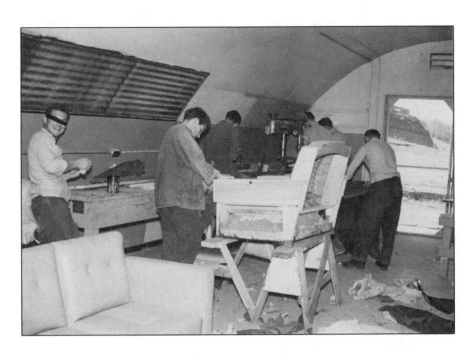

The Upholstery Shop.

West stood beside me with a knife in his hand. I would
mention, there were two knives — Inmate West had a
knife all the time. Inmate Turner then proceeded to
sharpen his knife on the grindstone. When he completed this they changed about. West went to the
grindstone and Turner came back to me. About this
time Turner went over to the phone and either cut or
broke the wires. Turner stood by me most of the
remainder of the time with West and Bird standing near
the opening cut in the door. During this period of time
I attempted to counsel these individuals and told them
how ridiculous it was. Turner said he had a lot of time
and the other two replied the same way and "nothing
was going to stop them." Turner said to me, "do not
try to play hero or try to warn them or you will have
this knife in your back."[8]

Shortly thereafter, the food and beverage truck approached the
shop, and the inmate-driver sounded his horn to alert the guard on the
outside that the morning tea had arrived. Officer Martin, who held the
shop keys, walked down from the Carpenter Shop to the Upholstery
Shop and looked inside the door's window to make a visual check.

He saw Instructor Uncles standing by the drill press, but thought nothing of it. As the armed guard opened the door to allow the tea container to be brought inside, he was grabbed by Inmate West, and had a knife held to his throat. West and Neil Turner, then disarmed him. Martin was forced at gunpoint to the back of the shop to where the other guard was. West, Turner, and Bird then rushed out the door.

As they exited the shop they ran up to the waiting delivery truck. Turner tried to open the door, but it was locked from the inside. Turner then pointed the revolver at the inmate-driver and fired. The bullet shattered the driver's side window, narrowly missing his face. He ducked down and was able to crawl out the passenger side of the cab and scramble across a field to safety. Turner ran to the back of the truck and stuck the muzzle of the gun into the face of the swamper inmate, who had been riding inside, watching the food. Turner ordered him to get off, and he too ran for cover.

The trio then commandeered the truck and they roared away from the Unit in a squeal of tires. They drove to the north end of the industrial shops and made a sharp left turn onto a service road that led to an unmanned gate on the west side of the property. The driver never slowed as he crashed through the large steel gate, ripping one side off its hinges. The driver's mirror shattered, with shards of glass flying in all directions, cutting up the face of one of the prisoners. The truck spun out onto Royal Oak Avenue, and the escapees drove down the hill for three blocks before abandoning it.

Brian Gallagher, 27, who lived on Buxton Street, saw the truck approaching as he was clearing the morning frost off the windshield of his 1963 Pontiac. The men got out in front of Gallagher's home and walked up to him. "The men looked tough," he later told a *Vancouver Sun* reporter.

> They got out of the truck and one of them stuck a
> revolver in my back and told me to get into the house.
> I had started my car up just before they arrived. It was
> running when they climbed out of the truck. The engine
> conked out and I watched them as they tried to start
> it. They finally got it going and they tore off down the
> street like madmen.[9]

The escapees then drove the stolen auto into Vancouver where they dumped it and stole another on West 12th Avenue. Two police officers spotted the men in the car near Main and Marine Drive and the chase was on. They followed the escapees at high speed through a maze of alleys and side streets. During the chase one of the bandits punched out the car's rear window and fired a shot at the officers. They abandoned the Pontiac at Victoria and Uplands with the police still hot on their trail. One of the officers fired a warning shot and then fired directly at one of the escapees as he saw him making his way in between houses, but the policeman only grazed the felon and he was able to continue on.

Bird was captured by police on the back porch of a home on Uplands Drive, and West was arrested a short distance away. Turner, however, was able to elude the police for the time being. Authorities cordoned off the area, and nearly sixty men, including twenty guards who were called to the scene, began the manhunt for him.

On receiving a report that a man matching Turner's description had entered a nearby school, the building was surrounded and police and guards waited with drawn guns for the school to be evacuated and searched. The search failed to find any trace of the fugitive.

Turner had walked to a home on Victoria Drive, where he entered the house and took a Mrs. Weber, and her 18-year-old and 2-year-old daughters hostage. The mother of nine later stated that, "when he walked in with his gun pointed at us, he seemed quite nervous at first. But he never made any direct threats except to say that he didn't care what he did because he had already shot somebody."[10]

The cool-headed woman was successful in keeping Turner calm and even prepared him some sandwiches. As the mother was expecting six of her children home shortly for lunch, the captive took the 18-year-old daughter upstairs, threatening the mother not to warn anyone of his whereabouts. Under the noise of running tap water, Mrs. Weber had one of her children phone and alert the police.

Soon the police had surrounded the house and were able to negotiate the convict into surrendering. Turner finally ended the daring escapade by handing over his gun to Mrs. Weber, once his safety had been guaranteed through the help of a *Vancouver Sun* reporter.

Escapee Wounded

In the spring of 1968, a 21-year-old convict, and another younger one, were among a group of twenty-five prisoners who had just finished participating in a Easter weekend program in the gymnasium. While armed guards were escorting them from the gym back to the Westgate Unit, the two suddenly made a dash for the west perimeter fence, nearly 100 metres away.

A guard yelled at them to stop, then drew his revolver and ran after them. When he saw the first reach the fence, he fired a warning shot over their heads. Neither of them stopped, so he fired another shot at both of them, not knowing if he had hit either one. One of the escapees climbed over the fence and crossed the street, the other decided to head north along the inside of the fence line so he could climb over further down. He ended up running into the arms of several guards.

Within a few minutes about twenty RCMP police officers, two tracking dogs, and a group of Oakalla guards began combing the area west of the prison for the one who had cleared the fence. An hour later the police were still having no luck with the dogs and darkness was hampering the search. Then a resident who lived several blocks away saw a man tumble into his neighbour's backyard. "He was staggering along behind the house and then he suddenly fell to the ground," he told a reporter. "I didn't know who he was for sure, but I knew the police were looking for somebody. So I hopped in my car and drove up the street a few blocks to get the police. I just told them that I thought I had found whoever they were looking for."[11]

The inmate had been hit in the back with a bullet from the guard's revolver, causing serious internal injury. He was taken to Vancouver General Hospital, underwent four hours of surgery, survived, and was later returned to Oakalla.

As might be expected, residents in the area were not only distraught over the escape, many were also concerned about potentially becoming innocent victims of shootings. Only six months later the surrounding community was again threatened by Oakalla escapees.

Wild Bid for Freedom
It was early Monday morning, October 7, 1968, when two guards, one armed with a shotgun and the other a .38 calibre handgun, were taking a group from the Westgate "B" Unit out to their work site on the prison grounds. As they escorted the men down a road, four convicts in their late teens quickly jumped the two guards. They viciously beat the officers as they desperately tried to retain their weapons. They were no match for the four youths, who successfully wrestled the shotgun and pistol away from them. They then took the weapons and ran towards the fence. By the time others had been informed of the escape, the young men had scaled the southeast property fence and were running through the streets of Burnaby looking for a means of escape.

The felons decided to steal a car, and they began to look for easy prey. First they ran to a home on nearby Berwick Street and knocked on the basement door. When the home owner answered the door one of the inmates pointed a gun at him and told him to "hold it." Almost

Leisure time in the Young Offenders' Unit.

instinctively, the man promptly slammed the door on the youth's face. The startled escapees ran off to try another target.

The fugitives then approached two girls who were walking down a street and ordered them to come with them to a nearby house. The girls saw the guns and ran into another home where they told a Mrs. Merritt what had just happened. She bolted the doors shut and phoned the police. Not having much luck, the escapees decided to split into pairs and approached separate homes.

Two of them, one of whom carried the revolver, burst into the home of Mrs. Lillian Bruce and took her as a hostage. One prisoner took some of her son's clothes and changed into them. The other took Lillian Bruce's clothing and proceeded to dress as a woman; make-up and all. The abductors then forced Bruce into her family car and headed out of the area.

In the meantime, the other two went to a home under construction next to the Bruce residence. In front of the house was a half-ton truck and the inmates found the owner inside laying brick for a fireplace. The bricklayer stated: "They came in and threatened to shoot if we did anything. They demanded the keys to the truck and I handed them over. It seemed that one couldn't drive and they had to switch the gun for the keys between them before they left."[12]

All local police departments were notified of the escape and road-blocks were set up at key locations. Less than half an hour later, the truck, loaded with limestone, was spotted by a New Westminster police officer at Eighth and McBride. The officer followed the truck at normal speeds over the Pattullo Bridge while waiting for reinforcements to join in. Once several other vehicles were in close proximity the police officer activated his lights and siren. Instead of pulling over the truck sped off and the chase was on. Police chased the vehicle at high rates of speed through Surrey and parts of Delta; at one point the truck swerved around a police roadblock. After a lengthy chase police managed to close in on the vehicle near the Deas Island Thruway, and boxed the suspects in with their cruisers. The two men finally surrendered to the police, leaving the shotgun on the floor of the truck.

Meanwhile, the two who had hijacked the Bruce car were driving through New Westminster when the car stalled at the intersection of Sixth Street and Sixth Avenue. Mr. Eccles was sitting in his 1967 Dodge at the same intersection and noticed three occupants in the red car in front of him. As he was deciding whether he should honk his horn or go around the stalled car, a woman ran from the car screaming for the police. Then a man dressed as a woman ran up to his car window, pointed a knife in his face, and told him to move over. Eccles was able to escape from his vehicle by falling out the passenger side of his car. He undid his seat belt, slid across the seat and opened the other door. When he did so he knocked some books onto the road, and as he went to pick them up, he rolled out of the car and made his way to safety.

Within minutes, police picked up the trail of the fugitives, chased them through the surrounding communities, but lost track of the suspect vehicle in the Delta area. A short time later, a Delta resident became suspicious of a car, with a shattered rear window, parked in front of his neighbour's home. Police surrounded the house and the prisoners, one still dressed in Bruce's clothing, were arrested. Their wild bid for freedom had lasted only four hours.

Murderous Attack on Guard
By the late 1960s Oakalla had become infamous for the turmoil within its walls. Part of the notoriety stemmed from the number of assaults on staff during that period. For example, the prison's 1966/67 Annual Report noted that there were sixty-one assaults on guards that year, ten of which were serious enough to warrant laying charges in outside court.

One of the most horrific attacks during the decade involved inmate Jaspert, a Francophone, who had been admitted to Oakalla in January 1969, remanded on murder and attempted murder charges. Almost immediately he began to cause problems for officials. On February 14, while a patient in the prison hospital, Jaspert had created a disturbance by swearing and threatening staff because a radio had been turned off. He told the guards that, "he was 'in for murder' and they (the staff) had better not push him around."[13]

Several weeks later, he was stopped by a West Wing guard while on his way to the exercise yard because he was carrying a number of blankets. The officer told him to return them to his cell, as it was against unit policy to bring them to the yard. The prisoner began swearing in French at the guard and at Officer Edmundson, who was standing nearby. Edmundson asked the prisoner why he wouldn't talk to him in English? Jaspert ignored the officer's comment, returned the blankets, and went out to the yard.

Three days later, on March 15, at the beginning of dayshift, Edmundson was walking down tier 5-Left, distributing the day's mail and "chasing" inmates off the tier for breakfast. As he entered the tier, Jaspert came out of his cell and gave Edmundson a "mean look." The officer ignored the stare and walked past him along the narrow walkway. As he walked by he felt a pain in his side and thought that Jaspert had punched him in the back. In fact, he had just been stabbed with a prison-made shiv. Edmundson turned around and saw Jaspert holding the bloody knife. He ordered him to drop the weapon, but Jaspert kept advancing on him. The prisoner then raised his knife and lunged at him. Edmundson grabbed the inmate's arm that was holding the knife as they fell to the floor. He could feel his strength draining while attempting to keep the blade of the knife away from his throat. As the two wrestled, Jaspert thrust the blade towards the officer's head and the tip inserted into his cheek, just below his left eye. At that moment back up staff arrived and disarmed Jaspert. The 28-year-old guard was rushed to Vancouver General Hospital. The puncture wound in his back had narrowly missed his heart. The Director of Corrections told reporters, "If the wound had been an inch over, it could have been fatal."[14]

Two days later, the Warden interviewed Jaspert from his Segregation cell. When Mulligan asked him why he stabbed Officer Edmundson, Jaspert simply replied that the guard had called him "yellow."

Until Jaspert was transferred to the Penitentiary, he continued to be a menace to the staff and management at Oakalla. He often made threats, wrote letters to members of the federal and provincial governments complaining of "cruel and unusual punishment," and was involved in assaults with both staff and other prisoners. Warden Mulligan once wrote: "At the present time I consider Jaspert to be one of the most highly dangerous prisoners I have known during my career in the Gaol Service."[15]

Guard Taken Hostage

Only several months after the attack on Edmundson, another guard's life was placed in serious jeopardy. In August 1969, a special security program was initiated where the most dangerous remand prisoners were held on tier 2-Left in the South Wing, (the old Death Row). This was developed so that staff could closely monitor violent inmates' movements, and place restrictions on them. Although they were housed in the same unit as the rest of the South Wing prisoners, they were kept virtually in solitary confinement. They were not allowed to go to the exercise yard, or to any other group event, with the rest of the prison population.

On March 8, 1969, inmate Collins was remanded to the prison on two "Non Capital Murder" and two "Attempt to Wound and Maim" charges. He was an extremely violent man who had a history of serving time in the penitentiary. On August 19, Collins attacked and stabbed another South Wing prisoner. As a result, he was placed on tier 2-Left. In late November his appeal to one of his murder charges ended and he was sentenced to life imprisonment.[16]

On November 24, Security Officer Beaupre, who had less than one year's experience, was scheduled to work the 3-11 afternoon shift in the South Wing and, as was his usual practice, he came to work approximately twenty minutes early. On his way into the Main Gaol he passed through the Centre Hall area and noticed that Collins was just finishing a visit. As a favour to the escorting officer, he took custody of the offender and brought him back into the South Wing. Beaupre searched him at the entrance to the unit and then escorted him up the stairs to the second landing. He then made a critical mistake, and breached unit policy, by going onto tier 2-Left without a back-up officer. The officer took Collins to his cell, but before he closed the cell-gate, Collins began to argue that he didn't have to be locked up as he was the only one on the tier. The officer agreed and turned to leave. As he was walking away, Collins said, "Mr. Beaupre, have a look at this." He turned around and started heading back when the inmate came out of his cell holding a honed table knife. Collins quickly encircled the officer, held the knife to his throat, and brought him back to his cell. He made him sit on the floor at the far end, and began to yell out that he had a hostage.

Minutes later, the Warden arrived and was met in the South Wing by the Deputy Warden and the Senior Medical Officer. The physician had just sent an oral sedative to the hostage, who was showing signs of anxiety. Collins allowed the officer to take the drug. Mulligan and the Deputy then proceeded down the tier to talk to the prisoner:

> As we advanced toward the cell Collins warned us not to come any closer (within approximately eight feet of the cell front). Collins was seated on the floor of his cell in the rear right hand corner between the toilet and the wall. Officer Beaupre was also seated on the floor between Collins' legs with his back in close contact with Collins' body. Collins had his left arm over Beaupre's left shoulder and around the officer's neck. The inmate was holding a crudely sharpened table knife in his right hand. The knife was held with the sharpened tip pointed at a spot on the side of the officer's neck just a few inches below the right ear.[17]

Collins told the Warden that he wished to see the Attorney-General and his own lawyer. He also stated that he was, "sick and tired of being locked up like a mad dog" and that he wanted to be treated like a human being. His basic demand was that he wanted the same freedoms and privileges as the other South Wing inmates, and he didn't want Oakalla's officials to tell the authorities at the B.C. Penitentiary that he had been violent while at Oakalla. Collins feared he would be immediately sent to "solitary" upon admission to the federal prison.

At 4:40 p.m. Mulligan contacted the Director of Correction and informed him of the crisis. They agreed that, to save the life of the guard, some concessions would have to be made. Mulligan returned to the scene and told Collins that if he released the hostage, they would allow him to leave the tier 2-Left security section and live with the rest of the South Wing. The Warden accepted that unless otherwise ordered, Collins would not be charged in relation to this incident (internally or in the courts), however, if he was charged with any further violations, he would be sent back to the security tier.

Collins was pleased with these conditions, however, he didn't trust the word of the Warden, and he wanted his lawyer present to witness this. The inmate's counsel was in Victoria and it would take hours to have him brought to Oakalla. Instead he agreed to have another

Warren H. Mulligan, Warden: 1963-1974.

Until the 1970s, Oakalla operated as a self-sufficient prison farm.

representative attend; one who lived in the Vancouver area. After a short wait the witness arrived and was taken to the South Wing. The Warden's agreement was then re-read, in the presence of the witness, and Collins released his hostage.

Yippies Invade Oakalla

Probably the strangest incident at Oakalla occurred not within the gaol but around the perimeter when a large group of young protestors attempted an "invasion" of the prison on July 12, 1970.

On July 1, the *Georgia Straight* newspaper ran an article by a radical group calling itself the Vancouver Liberation Front, which called for the dismantling of institutions, like Oakalla, which held "political prisoners." The article stated they were planning a "be-in" at the prison. Several days later, their rhetoric became more militant and they demanded that on July 12, Oakalla be demolished and all prisoners be pardoned. A spokesman said, "a very large portion of people are in prison for victimless crimes — dope, attempted suicide, vagrancy. Others are in for petty economic crimes. If you break into a phone box for the small change, you are liable for quite a long time in prison."[18]

Deputy Warden Bellis and an inspector with the Burnaby RCMP formulated a plan to ensure the security of the prison. The police would be responsible for developments outside the fence and Oakalla guards would stand at the ready inside the perimeter to apprehend any trespassers. The potential for fires being set was also discussed and the Burnaby Fire Department would be called to stand-by.

On the morning of July 12, all Oakalla personnel, except those on leave or working the graveyard shift, reported to the prison. The parking lot was cleared of vehicles, in case they were damaged by looting or riot. Forty-five RCMP officers were brought into the prison and kept out of sight, to be called only if an emergency situation developed. That morning, inmate program went ahead as usual, except for the cancellation of visits.

In the early afternoon, the Yippies assembled at Forest Glen Park, about five blocks from the prison. Nearly 300 young men and women gathered there to listen to radical speeches, dance, sing, and smoke marijuana. A live band provided music and some of the girls went onstage and danced topless, to the delight of the crowd.

At 7:45 p.m. the protestors left the park and marched in unison a half-mile to an open field at the south-west corner of the prison property. They were not met with a show of force, but rather about five RCMP officers. There were more political speeches, then some of the youths jumped up on one of the fences and began to shake it. They found a weak link and a group of about fifty joined in and worked together in pulling at the wire mesh until they had torn down a section nearly 100 metres long. Once the fence was down, approximately a dozen youths ventured onto the prison property.

By this time the squads of police and correctional officers had been deployed to the area. Eighty guards carrying riot equipment were sent to the parking lot to prevent the crowd from advancing any further, while fifty unarmed RCMP Officers marched up Royal Oak hill and proceeded along the fence line. Upon seeing the show of force, the protestors backed off and retreated into the tall grass field.

A stand-off developed, with the protestors yelling obscenities and taunting the line of RCMP. Some of the Yippies lit fireworks and sent them hurtling into the prison grounds hoping to set fires, but they burned out without causing damage. After about an hour, the crowd decided to return to the park for more speeches and entertainment. Although the police and prison staff maintained a vigil throughout the night, the radicals never returned as a group to Oakalla.

All livestock were removed from Oakalla during the mid-1970s.

Oakalla the Warehouse

In April 1970, the Provincial Legislature passed the *Correction Act,* which incorporated a new ideology towards penology. The old "medical model" approach was abandoned, as it was seen as a general failure in trying to rehabilitate offenders. Many criminals left prison more dangerous and violent than when they were first admitted. The new theme was the "Re-integration Model," which no longer saw inmates as being "sick," but responsible for their crimes. One of this ideal's key elements was to divert the majority of offenders away from prison, and to assist in re-integrating them back into society.

Since many inmate programs were now directed outside the walls of prisons and within the community, the result at Oakalla was a closure of most of its work and treatment programs, due to a lack of funding. Even though the prison's overall population dramatically dropped, as high numbers were given early parole or sent to half-way houses, those who remained were a stagnant group of hard-core offenders who were unfit for community placement.

In accordance with the new policy, Oakalla was no longer going to be run as a farm, since it wasn't cost effective, and few prisoners would be looking for work in agriculture once released. Therefore, "Oakalla Prison Farm" was officially renamed the "Lower Mainland Regional Correctional Centre," and, over the next four years, all farming operations were closed. The award-winning Clydesdale team was moved to Fort Steele, crops were no longer planted, the piggery and dairy were closed, more than 150 head of livestock were removed from the farm, and most of the industrial shops closed.

During Mulligan's final years he helplessly watched government legislation turn back the clock on Oakalla, creating a prison atmosphere resembling the pre-rehabilitation years. As in the late 1940s, there was once again virtually no work at the prison; there were few educational or treatment programs; and the wings were full of violent men. A further critical problem was that as other smaller correctional institutions attempted to keep their policies in line with this new approach, they dealt with their difficult prisoners by transferring them to Oakalla. The Warden often complained that Oakalla had become the "dumping grounds" for the other prisons:

> The Lower Mainland Regional Correctional Centre still must play the role of the "last resort Centre" to deal with the Province's criminally orientated anti-social and sociopathic persons. The Centre also continues to house our physically and mentally impaired persons who are seriously deteriorated from alcohol and drug abuse. These people cannot be rehabilitated or placed back in society's stream but require a constant nursing type of care.[19]

Only a few years after the "Re-integration Model" was introduced, prison officials began to realize the detrimental consequences it had on Oakalla. They conceded that while the community approach had some positive effect on convicts who qualified for such programs, there was still a significant proportion who required custody. Although the Corrections Branch was now concerned with the lack of activities for them, it would take several years before any meaningful developments were reinstated.

Seven

Years of Destruction
1974-1987

When Henry B. Bjarnason transferred from Prince George Regional Correctional Centre in October 1974, to run Oakalla, he inherited a situation where few improvements had been made over the previous four years and tension remained dangerously high. Just a year before, on September 29, 1973, Westgate exploded in a near-riot. A large group of prisoners went on a rampage, crashing through the walls of two tiers, smashing tables, throwing chairs, and attempting to free other locked-up inmates. They were eventually suppressed when officers turned fire hoses on them. Earlier in the year, there had been several arson attacks. In June, an inmate was charged with causing $85,000 in damage when the barn was torched; in May 700 swine went up in smoke during another spectacular blaze.

Shortly after Bjarnason took over, the government introduced its first Five Year Plan for Corrections. One of the objectives was to replace Oakalla with a number of smaller facilities, and officials decided to start the phase-out by closing Westgate. However, at this stage, there weren't even blueprints for the new prisons, and not all the prisoners in Westgate could be allocated into other wings or centres; so it remained open. In July 1975, a community-based group

The piggery closed in 1973, when 700 swine perished in a spectacular blaze.

called the Prisoners' Union Committee (PUC), helped organize a protest staged by nearly 150 Westgate and East Wing offenders on the upper ball field, following a sports day. As the prisoners demanded job training and improved living conditions, PUC members distributed pamphlets to reporters and curious citizens who had assembled to watch the stand-off. The inmates refused to return to their cells that night, and it wasn't until noon the following day, when fifty guards donned riot gear and prepared to storm the field, that they surrendered.

Before Bjarnason's arrival, a change in policy required Oakalla to hold all prisoners waiting trial who had been remanded for psychological evaluations. Previously, these had been conducted at Riverview Hospital. In one year, more than 400 such evaluations were conducted, creating an enormous strain.[1] These men did not mix in well with the others, and Oakalla's noisy environment was hardly the place to conduct assessments. Outbreaks of self-inflicted and other forms of violence began to occur. On May 7, 1975, William Sackville, a 22-year-old transient, was found hanging by a bedsheet in his cell. He had been charged with the first-degree murder of a young Simon Fraser University secretary, whose partially clad body was found tied spread-eagle to a bed, with her throat slit.[2] Several months later,

124

July 2, 1975, stand-off, upper ball field.

Louise Lewicki hanged herself in the waiting trial ward of the Women's Centre. She had been committed for trial for the murder of "Big Shorty" Garcean, who had been found in his rooming-house room with his feet bound and multiple stab wounds in his back.[3]

In 1978, the Warden finally saw some requests for change met when the Corrections Branch announced that approval had been given for construction of the $18-million Vancouver Pre-trial Centre. Together, this building and a proposed second facility, were to completely eliminate Oakalla's remand population. Corrections also announced that, over the next few years, two 150-bed, secure facilities for sentenced inmates would be constructed and Oakalla would definitely be closed by the mid-1980s. In the meantime, "temporary measures" would be implemented until the new gaols could be built.

In June 1979, most of the industrial shops were re-opened, and a number of educational and psychological services were also re-instated. Fewer inmates were paroled, put on probation, or given temporary absence passes. After almost a decade of warehousing prisoners, positive steps had finally been undertaken to bring it to an end. By the early 1980s almost half of the prison's sentenced population was actively employed in some work or educational program. Most of the remaining unemployed sentenced prisoners were housed in the East Wing, where the cramped quarters and need for high security limited access to activities.

Sex Scandal

In late 1977, public attention was drawn to the Oakalla Women's Correctional Centre, following allegations of sexual misconduct between male guards and female inmates. On October 25, the first report of wrongdoing was aired by an ex-inmate on a CKNW radio talk-show hosted by Jack Webster. Two allegations were made: An officer had been forced to resign after being involved in an operation to smuggle gold jewellery into the women's prison from Hong Kong; and three male guards had been demoted for having sexual relations with female prisoners.[4] The Commissioner of Corrections responded by promising that an internal investigation would begin immediately. But as the days passed the media reported further allegations. At first the Corrections Branch attempted to brush off these reports; however, as they grew both in number and seriousness — criminal activity was often suggested — the government had no choice but to call for a full-scale public inquiry. The Inquiry began in January 1978, with Madam Justice Proudfoot appointed as sole commissioner. During the investigation, staff and prisoners pointed out a number of contributing factors which may have precipitated it.

One of the problems noted was lack of clear leadership and management at the Centre. From 1972 to 1977, the facility was under several male directors, who were often seconded to the position, or placed there temporarily. At the same time the women's prison struggled, unsuccessfully, to be autonomous from the men's institution.

Even more disruptive was the crisis generated by the introduction of male staff in 1975. Although there had been several male supervisors at the centre before, no men actually worked in the living units. The trouble began when the Haney Correctional Centre closed. Most of the male guards were transferred to other institutions; however, only so many positions could be absorbed by these facilities. In an agreement between management and the employees' union, male guards — who had more seniority — were able to bump matrons at the Women's Centre from their positions. In conjunction, the Human Rights Branch had recently recommended that women be allowed to work as guards in the male institution and *vice versa,* providing that "human decency and privacy were not affected." Within two years, some twenty male officers were assigned to work in the women's living units, providing security, searching living quarters, counselling women, and escorting them on day-passes. It wasn't long before problems arose, and a joint union-management committee was set up in late 1977 to study them. Before their findings were documented, rumours of immorality were being headlined in local newspapers.

Prior to the Inquiry being called, two former matrons went public claiming that a female prisoner had died while a doctor, who was in the prison at the time, refused to come to her aid. One of the ex-matrons said that the prison doctor was only feet away, in his office having a cup of tea, while the prisoner lay dying from a drug overdose. She also claimed that the doctor was called on to help on three occasions (twice by herself), but he refused. The woman stated that she quit over the cover-up, adding that she was never given the opportunity to supply this information when the inmate's death was investigated at the Coroner's Inquest.[5]

The first allegation was based on the rumour that an officer had been forced to resign after he had placed an order with an inmate's relative in Hong Kong to have $1600 in gold jewellery sent to her. The officer and three other staff members were buying the items for themselves and depositing the purchase price in the inmate's prison account. The Inquiry found that although five guards had actually been involved, only two had been reprimanded. None had been forced to resign (one guard had quit over another matter). As it turned out, the jewellery never got to Oakalla. It was stopped at the border by Canadian Customs, with more than $400 in duty owing. In the end the merchandise was returned to the sender. Although it was not a criminal act to carry on business transactions with prisoners, an officer who did so was certainly violating the "Gaol Rules and Regulations."

The second rumour was that three guards had been demoted for having sex with a female prisoner. When police attempted to locate the woman to confirm the story, they found she had since died of a drug overdose in Vancouver. Also no guard had been demoted in relation to this allegation.

One of the most serious allegations reported to the press was that a male officer had escorted a female inmate to Vancouver on a day-pass, taken her to a hotel where they drank and had sexual intercourse, and later allowed her to escape.[6] The Inquiry revealed that the allegation was not far from the truth. When interviewed by police, the former inmate stated that she and the officer had arrived at a woman friend's apartment in the early afternoon. She and her friend sat together drinking beer, while the officer had tea. She remembered him telling her not to get drunk. She then asked her friend to go out on the street and buy some drugs. The friend left, made no effort to buy any narcotics, and later returned saying that she couldn't get any. The two women were soon out of beer, so they asked the guard to lend them five dollars to buy more. According to the ex-inmate, he gave her the money and soon began falling asleep. After they returned with the liquor, the ex-inmate excused herself to use the washroom and escaped through the bathroom window. When the guard realized she was gone, he telephoned the institution and fabricated a story of how the inmate had given him the slip while they were in a restaurant. During the interview, the escapee told police that she picked this particular officer for the day-pass because she considered him a "good friend." However, she denied any sexual involvement with him.

When questioned by the police, the officer stated that he escorted the prisoner to a Vancouver restaurant. From there they went to the apartment, where he allowed her to drink some beer. He denied any sexual involvement with her, but did remember her giving him a kiss in the apartment. He said that he had not fallen asleep, but that the escape occurred when he allowed the two women to leave the apartment to get some "fresh air."[7]

A story was also brought forward that a male guard had taken a female prisoner to the Isolation Unit to have sex, where they were discovered by another guard *flagrante delicto*. When questioned by the RCMP, the officer who reportedly had come upon the incident, said that he had found the two in the unauthorized area, but saw no overt sexual activity. Other guards noticed that the two were particularly friendly, however — so it may have come as no surprise that when the woman was released from prison, she and the guard got married.[8]

Although the Inquiry found some truth to a number of other stories, such as the male guard who routinely searched the female prisoners' underwear hampers, the majority of rumours were found to be false or unsupported.[9] The scope of the Inquiry went beyond these allegations, and focused on many other concerns surrounding women offenders. The Commissioner's report listed a total of fifty-seven recommendations to improve conditions at the prison, relating to changes to: programming, facilities, inmate rights, and staffing. The most notable recommendation, to eliminate men from the women's living units, was quickly implemented.

Civilian Taken Hostage

Back at the men's prison, order was once again interrupted by another grave hostage-taking incident on December 27, 1978. Twenty-two-year-old Dewey Sigo, a dangerous American escapee from Walla Walla Penitentiary in Washington State, where he was serving fifteen years for robbery, was apprehended on the streets of Vancouver in November and taken to Oakalla on an immigration hold. On that December morning, two immigration officers and Court Reporter Elsie Wanless, 58, were brought into the visiting area of the prison for Sigo's Extradition Hearing.

Mrs. Wanless was busily taking notes when Sigo got up from where he was sitting and threw his arm around her neck. He produced a weapon fashioned from the blade of a hobby knife, held it to her throat, and ordered the two officers to leave the room.

When prison officials received word of the hostage-taking, a special RCMP tactical unit was called in. One of the members, Corporal Leach, an experienced hostage negotiator, spent the next four hours trying to convince the prisoner to abandon his demands for better treatment and living conditions at Oakalla, while armed marksmen stood poised in the background. The negotiator played on the age of the slightly crippled hostage, hoping the prisoner would have some sympathy for her. He reminded Sigo that if he harmed the elderly woman he would not be supported by his fellow prisoners and would likely require protective custody. Leach later told reporters: "I told Sigo that if he had seized a young man as a hostage, his fellow prisoners might rally around him, but that he wouldn't gain any sympathy by using an older woman.... 'There's no glory in taking a mother-image hostage.'"[10] The standoff continued for several more hours and, although the hostage broke down and cried a number of times, she never panicked. Just after 5:00 p.m., more than seven hours after the ordeal began, Sigo released his shaken hostage and surrendered. Following this incident, a special cage was installed in the visiting area where high-security inmates would sit during hearings and interviews.

Two Wings Riot

In Oakalla's violent history, the 1980s proved to be more destructive than all other decades combined. For years, inmates had been promised new facilities — but little had in fact changed and the old gaol continued to deteriorate.

Several significant events preceded the February 1980 disturbances. In late December 1979, and early January 1980, there was a major disturbance at the women's section of the prison. At 9:30 p.m. on New Year's Eve a group of women staged a sit-in protest on the second floor of the Main Building. The sit-in turned into a minor riot when the women went on a destructive rampage and barricaded themselves in a room. After thirteen hours the stand-off ended when the matrons and male officers tore down the barricades and removed the rebellious prisoners to the Isolation Unit underneath the old Cow Barn.

Fourteen women were sentenced to various lengths of solitary confinement. In the "hole," they decided that they were being subject

In the 1950s, there were few incidents of bloodshed. Here a community softball team makes a "double play" against an East Wing team.

to "cruel and unusual punishment" because of the deplorable conditions, and staged another sit-in, right there in Isolation. When staff attempted to send some of them back to their regular cells, they refused to budge. There were no plumbing fixtures in these cells, and the women had to relieve themselves in plastic buckets. On one occasion, when matrons opened their cell doors, some of the women threw buckets of excrement at them. Marie Peacock, Director of the Women's Unit, gave the prisoners a three-day "cooling-off" period before taking further action. She ordered the matrons to enter the unit only to deliver food and perform other essential duties. She stated, "I don't want any more of my staff getting human excretion dumped on them.... It was a degrading experience, I can tell you, to get hit like that."[11]

Although there were other contributing factors, the event that actually sparked the riots occurred far from the gates of Oakalla. On February 2, 1980, the eyes and ears of the world tuned into the state prison at Santa Fe, New Mexico. Next to the 1971 prison riot at Attica, New York, this was the largest and most violent riot witnessed in North American penal history. In two days, more than 1,000 prisoners held and tortured twelve prison guards, burned down a large part of the prison, and went on a murderous rampage killing thirty-nine inmates who were labelled as being either sex offenders or "snitches." It was more than mere coincidence that, only three days after the Santa Fe rioting began, disturbances started at Oakalla.

The turmoil began around 8:00 p.m. on February 5, when a group of South Wing inmates refused to return to their respective tiers following a period of inside "yard" on the bottom tier. Principal Officer Tkachuk telephoned Deputy Director Hofseth and informed him that twenty-eight prisoners were refusing a direct order. The Deputy asked that three inmates, to act as spokesmen, be brought into the South Wing office. They cited the following list of grievances:

1: South Wing Unit is in a filthy state.
2: Cleaners serving food are dirty and not medically cleared.
3: No standard policy in Unit.
4: No action taken on medical requirements.
5: Director's Court is pre-judged.
6: Request for regular visits to be lengthened.
7: Late returnees from court always receive cold food.[12]

Hofseth advised the men he couldn't deal with these issues immediately and asked the prisoners to return to their cells. They refused. After contacting Warden Bjarnason, Hofseth decided against a confrontation and allowed the prisoners to remain where they were for the night. Fifteen members of the afternoon-shift were kept on as extra security throughout the night and all day-shift staff were advised to report early for work.

The prisoners remained quiet all night, however, and as promised, at 6:30 a.m. Hofseth and the Warden met with the spokesmen and went over the grievances. The inmates were told that they would be given no immediate answers, but the Warden would have a written statement answering all their concerns prepared within three hours. The two officials then left to prepare their statement.

The prisoners were not prepared to wait. Shortly after the officials left, they smashed tables and chairs and tried to barricade the entrance. A large group of guards were sent onto the tier, regained control with minimal force, and returned the offenders to their individual cells. The only injury during the scuffle was to a prisoner, who required several stitches after a guard accidentally kicked a piece of glass off the overhead cat-walk, striking him on the head some twenty feet below.

Throughout the day, the South Wing remained peaceful as the prisoners cleaned up their mess, but shortly after 8:00 p.m. the West Wing started its own disturbance. The Deputy Director ran to the second landing to see what all the noise was about. He saw about seventy prisoners on tier 1-Right breaking windows, tables, and benches, and pulling on the steam pipes, which came crashing to the floor. As dense steam filled the entire right side of the Unit, the order was given to have the other wings locked-down and all on-duty staff report to the West Wing. Officers armed with shotguns were deployed to surround the outer perimeter and staff on the inside grabbed firehoses. However, the guards did not venture onto the tiers, where steam had reduced visibility to zero. By 8:30 p.m. the fifty convicts on the left side of the bottom tier had also joined in the disturbance and extra chains and locks were brought in to secure the end-gates on all the tiers. Once again Bjarnason asked for three inmate spokesmen.

Negotiations began around 10:00 p.m., and continued until shortly before 6:00 a.m., when the prisoners requested that lawyer J. Mackrow assist them. He arrived around 9:00 a.m., and just over an hour later, after receiving assurances that their concerns would be seriously investigated, the 120 prisoners agreed to return to their cells. For the remainder of the day the two wings remained quiet.

On the following day, just before the dinner hour, prison officials caught wind that convicts were planning to rush a guard and take a hostage. The guards decided to serve dinner as usual, albeit cautiously, to prevent an incident. After dinner had been served, and the inmates were locked in their cells, management decided to play it safe and keep them locked up for the remainder of the night.

It didn't take long for inmates to start acting up once they realized they weren't going to be released. Many complained that the authorities had broken a promise to allow routine programs to resume if they remained peaceful. Shortly after 6:00 p.m., several prisoners began banging on their cell bars, and it didn't take long before the majority joined in, and the Wing was in a complete uproar. A couple of felons on tier 3-Right threw their bedding and other material out of their cells and set them on fire. Others smashed up their cells. At 6:20 p.m. Deputy Director Hofseth ordered staff onto the cat-walks and directed them to use the fire hoses on any inmate who was breaking property. The guards had to dodge porcelain missiles as they proceeded along the narrow planks, during a rampage that lasted for over forty-five minutes before the hoses managed to douse inmate aggression.

At 7:15 p.m. staff moved onto tier 1-Right and began to remove inmates who were found with damaged property in their cells. One by one they were taken and escorted outside to the paddy wagon, which dropped them off at the stairs leading down to the punishment cells beneath the Cow Barns. A total of fifty-eight prisoners were removed and crammed into the segregation cells.

In the afternoon of the following day, a thorough search of the West Wing was conducted. Sifting through the soaked rubble, guards uncovered ten weapons fashioned from bed-legs and pipes. They also discovered a small knife, honed from a metal spoon. "What we found indicated that our information about a hostage-taking was probably right," Warden Bjarnason later told reporters.[13]

The total damage ran to more than $50,000, with an additional $10,000 spent on overtime expenses. Fifty-three inmates were subsequently charged in provincial court with damaging government property.

Explaining the roots of the riot, Bjarnason restated an all-too-familiar cause: "The basic problem... is that the West Wing houses only prisoners on remand — waiting to go to trial — and the cellblock lacks adequate facilities to help them pass the weeks and even months they sometimes have to wait."[14] However, he failed to take into consideration that attention was focused on prisons everywhere because of the violent riot at New Mexico's State Penitentiary, and Oakalla's inmates took advantage of the opportunity to publicize their grievances. One can also suggest that, as Oakalla inmates heard stories of the guards being held and brutally molested in Santa Fe, some of them saw this as a chance to pay back their own guards.

Prisoners Shot

July 7, 1980, was warm and sunny, and thirty-six South Wing inmates seemed to be enjoying a few hours of afternoon yard when something caught a tower guard's attention. He noticed that several prisoners had moved a weight bench from one area of the yard and set it in front of an outdoor urinal. Suddenly six of them used the bench to climb on top of the urinal and scramble up a vent-pipe that ran up the outside wall of the East Wing. With lightning speed they scaled the high fence and jumped onto the roof of the Classi-

Fire hoses were often used to quell major disturbances.

Another manhunt for escapees begins.

fication Unit.

As the first prisoner landed on the roof, the guard in the tower yelled at the pack to stop. No one heeded his warning, so he pumped a round into his shotgun and fired a warning shot over their heads. They ignored the blast and kept running along the roof. At this point the officer decided to shoot directly at the three who were furthest from him. He likely missed, for they continued to make their way across the roof.

A second guard, patrolling along the road in front of the South Wing yard heard the other officer's shouts and gunfire. He saw the escapees on the roof and ordered them to stop. After firing his own warning shot, he also attempted to gun them down. As before, the small-calibre pellets only took a little steam out of them. By this time all six prisoners had climbed down from the roof and were running across the prison grounds, with armed staff close behind.

The second officer then saw a seventh inmate attempting to escape by scaling the yard fence. He warned the prisoner to stop, and then — finding that he was down to his last round — fired a shot directly at him. The blast hit the inmate in the buttocks, incapacitating him.

The other escapees were soon re-captured. Some were found near the upper ball field, others by the West Wing, and one was tracked to his hiding place on the grounds by an RCMP dog. The escapee who had been shot directly had to be taken to a local hospital, while the others were treated at the prison's facilities and returned to their cells.

The incident did not end at this point. The twenty-nine inmates left in the South Wing yard felt that excessive force had been used to prevent the escape. At 8:30 p.m. they advised officials that, in protest, they were refusing to return to their cells. In response, extra security staff were assigned to patrol the perimeter of the Wing, and the other units were locked down. The Warden later reported that the inmates penned in the yard became riotous before guards in the other wings had a chance to lock up their charges:

> Before we could achieve this, South Wing inmates [in the yard] commenced climbing East Wing walls and started smashing windows in the East Wing which prompted the East Wing inmates to start yelling, smashing and banging their cell doors. South Wing yard inmates continued their rampage. Extra staff were called in, riot equipment issued to staff and fire hoses were strung out. Inmates were given the opportunity to come in from the yard and refused to do so. Fire hoses were used shortly after.[15]

Meanwhile, in Westgate "B", nearly forty prisoners began to trash their cells. Although damage was minimal, their actions prevented the Westgate staff from assisting their co-workers in the Main Gaol. At the same time, ten inmates housed on the right side of the East Wing smashed their toilets.

Two hours later, a pair of representatives from the yard met with officials to discuss their grievances. The inmates were informed that, although several offenders had been shot, none was seriously wounded, and the RCMP would be conducting a thorough investigation into the incident. Satisfied, the pair convinced the others to return to their cells.

Olson in Oakalla

No higher security classification was afforded to any other prisoner than Clifford Olson, who had confessed to the murders of ten children. By the time he was brought to Oakalla, in September 1981, he was not only the constant focus of the media and an outraged public, but also the scorn of the inmate population, from whom he had to be protected.

Tier locking system.

Olson was placed in the second cell on the right side of the South Wing Observation Unit. His only furnishing was a mattress on the floor. There were five cells on this side of the tier; however, during his initial incarceration, he was housed with only two other prisoners. Olson soon complained to the media about his treatment. He stated that he had to "live like a dog," sleeping on the floor with no bedding, lights, or running water. He also claimed that he was a target of physical and verbal abuse from guards and inmates, and that the other prisoners on his tier would throw water, garbage, and lighted cigarettes at him.[16] The Director of the South Wing responded to the allegations by calling Olson a "chronic complainer," and stated that he wouldn't be getting special treatment in Observation. However, when Olson's lawyer raised his client's concerns in court, the provincial Ombudsman was asked to investigate. During the one-week inquiry, Olson was taken from Oakalla and held in the Burnaby RCMP lock-up.

The Ombudsman concluded that, although some profanity had been directed towards Olson, his treatment was "adequate and normal." The child murderer still feared that other prisoners might attempt to kill him, so Corrections officials decided that he would be kept alone on the tier, and that whenever he had to leave his cell for prison visits or court appearances, those areas of the gaol he had to pass through on his way would be locked down.

His continuing presence meant that for months there was no space available to segregate emotionally and mentally disturbed inmates who would otherwise have been held in the Observation Unit. Olson was transferred from Oakalla to a special unit in Kingston Penitentiary on February 17, 1982, where he remains today.

South Wing Erupts Again

Another major disturbance ignited at the troubled prison in September 1982. At the time the South Wing was dominated by a formidable group of "heavies," high-profile inmates who represented extra responsibility for Warden Bjarnason and caused problems for both staff and other prisoners.

Near the end of day-shift at 2:30 p.m. on Sunday, September 19, the South Wing yard was called in, but the twenty-eight inmates in the yard refused to comply and staged a sit-in. Shortly after 3:30 p.m., Mr. Hofseth (who was now the Local Director of the South Wing) was contacted at home and asked to come in and speak to the prisoners. Once at the prison he asked for two spokesmen to be brought in from the yard.

The two who volunteered were handcuffed and escorted to Hofseth's office. They made only one request: the return of four inmates who had been found under the influence of an unknown substance and sent to the Segregation Unit the day before. He denied their request. He advised the Warden of the sit-in, and as a result, portable lighting was brought in to illuminate the yard, fire hoses were strung out, and the RCMP were called in to secure the outside of the institution.

At 6:00 p.m., East Wing inmates were locked in their cells to allow for additional cover of the South Wing. Some inmates in the South Wing yard then climbed onto a ledge that looked into the East Wing, and began to taunt prisoners there into creating a disturbance. The Warden later outlined the ensuing incident:

> At approximately 6:55 p.m. the fire hoses were attached to the hydrants and inmates were hosed off the ledge of the right side of the East Wing as they had already commenced hollering at inmates in the wing and smashing windows. The inmates in South Wing yard continued their disturbance by smashing benches and tables in the yard and commenced ramming the outside yard steel door. The door started to bulge and

at this critical point, Principal Officer MacCubbin fired three rounds of ammunition to prevent what could have been a mass exit from the yard.[17]

After two more hours of harassment, some East Wing prisoners began to destroy their cells. Extra staff were called in from other units, but there was little they could do as prisoners pulled sinks from the walls and smashed toilets. There were too few staff available to deal with the disturbance effectively, as many of them were trying to handle the situation in the South Wing yard. Destruction of the East Wing continued for another two hours before staff regained control. Thirty-two convicts were later removed from their cells and sent to the Westgate "A" Segregation Unit to await disciplinary action. The South Wing prisoners had smashed more than 100 panes of glass along the East Wing wall, while the East Wing inmates had demolished a similar number of wash basins, toilets, and desks.

In the meantime, for no apparent reason, some inmates in the South Wing yard began to beat another inmate viciously. He managed to scramble to safety on the ledge of the East Wing wall, where he stayed until several South Wing inmates talked him into coming down, assuring his safety. As soon as he was back inside the yard, three others jumped him and once again began to assault him. At this point, Officer MacCubbin drew his .38 calibre revolver and fired another warning shot over the assailants' heads. The startled gang retreated momentarily, giving the victim enough time to once again climb onto the ledge. He then begged the staff surrounding the yard to help him and began to climb up the yard fence from the ledge. Hofseth ordered the officers to hold their fire and allow the inmate to crawl over the fence. As he made his way up the chain link fence, South Wing prisoners fired the smashed debris that was strewn about the yard at him. He got over the fence safely, but fell on the other side and broke an ankle. He was then taken into custody and sent to the Health Care Centre for examination.

The disturbance continued late into the evening, and the rebellious group put forward a number of demands. Most importantly, they wanted to be allowed to return to their cells in the South Wing and not to be sent to Segregation for punishment. The Warden rejected their request, fearing that they would also destroy their cells once back inside. The confrontation lasted until after 1:00 a.m. Then staff were called into the yard to begin removing the hostile prisoners, and Bjarnason gave the order to re-open the Old Isolation Unit underneath the Cow Barn, as the Segregation Unit in Westgate "A" was currently filled with prisoners from the East Wing. Within an hour all the group had been frisked and secured in the O.I.U. There were no further disruptions that night.

Third Bullet Downs Prisoner

On August 14, 1983, twenty-year-old inmate Marvin Joe was shot several times during an attempted escape — and survived. Joe, having served half his one-year sentence for theft, scaled a fence around an exercise yard and was running across the property when he was spotted heading towards the perimeter fence. The officer who was watching the yard yelled at him several times to stop. As he continued to flee, the guard drew his service revolver and fired a warning shot. Joe kept on running. The guard then drew down on the escapee and fired one shot, hitting him in the arm. The prisoner hardly lost a pace.

A second officer saw the escape and also fired a warning shot, again without success. He then fired his .38 calibre revolver directly at Joe, striking him in the chest. The wounded man had such drive that even this did not stop him. Finally, a third shot which struck Joe in the neck brought him down. He was rushed to Vancouver General Hospital where he underwent emergency surgery, eventually recovered, and was returned to the prison. It had been his second escape attempt in ten weeks.

Oakalla's Worst Riot

On August 2, 1983, more than 100 remand inmates were taken from the West Wing and bussed to the newly opened Vancouver Pretrial Services Centre (VPSC). Before the Centre's opening, the Warden had planned to ease overcrowding by using the West Wing to house all remand prisoners, and free-up beds in the East and South Wings for sentenced men. However, when VPSC opened, Bjarnason had to abandon his plan. It fell victim to economic restraint, and a requirement to overhaul sub-standard fire safety equipment in the Wings of the Main Gaol. The Fire Marshal had been demanding new fire exit doors and an alarm system for years. The Warden was pressured into sending all prisoners from the East and South Wings to the now-vacant West Wing, which would allow technicians to upgrade the other two Wings and at the same time reduce Oakalla's operating costs. (The West Wing had previously been renovated with the new alarm system). This seemed to be a waste of money. A report into the ensuing riot stated: "It seemed counterproductive for the Branch to expend 3.4 million dollars on fire safety upgrading and then close two of those Wings for economic reasons."[18] Prison officials, however, maintained that the population of Oakalla was in constant fluctuation and the Wings should be upgraded because of the likelihood of having to re-open them in the future. By mid-November, South Wing remand inmates and sentenced East Wing inmates were housed together in the West Wing. The mix did not sit well with either staff or prisoners.

In the "inmate code" there are rules of social status that are foreign to the outside world. On the criminal social ladder, those imprisoned for murder and serious crimes, or those who have survived years in the violent world of the penitentiary system, cling to the top rung and are considered the institution's "heavies." Much lower on the status ladder are inmates who are serving relatively short sentences or are young and inexperienced in prison. The bottom rung is saved for sex offenders and finks or "rats." They require protective custody, apart from the general prison population.

When the transfer occurred, South Wing prisoners were generally the "heavies," while many East Wingers were "young noisy punks" who didn't know how to "do time." A report into the riot noted that there were occasional arguments between the two groups, once they were in the wing together: "Much of this [verbal] interaction involved arguments over 'the young punks' making too much noise on the tier and hostile arguments centred on 'turf', with the weights room as an example."[19]

The tension created by blending remand and sentenced prisoners was obvious, and both prisoners and staff predicted a disturbance. Ted Harrison, the Regional Director of Corrections, told reporters, only days before the riot, that he had received a telephone call from a prisoner who was worried about the explosive situation in the Wing. Harrison said: "We had warnings signs but, in their wisdom, the directors felt these signs weren't sufficiently grave to warrant preventive measures."[20]

The "tinderbox" was ready to ignite, and on Tuesday, November 22, 1983, a series of events sparked it. At 9:25 a.m., Correctional Officers Davis and Wasson brought a plumber onto tier 3-Left, to repair toilets. One cell requiring attention was occupied by inmate Movold who refused to be locked in another cell while the plumber fixed his toilet. Davis took the inmate by the arm and was escorting him out of the cell when he turned and punched the officer in the face, breaking his nose. As Davis attempted to recover, Movold continued to strike blows to his face and body. Inmate White joined in and kicked the guard in the groin. As Wasson attempted to assist his fellow officer, Movold broke free from the struggle and ran into his cell where he picked up an iron bed leg and swung it around wildly, threatening the two men. Seeing that they had no immediate back-up, the guards retreated off the tier. Other officers quickly took over and disarmed Movold. Fearing that they might trigger a disturbance, staff decided not to send the two prisoners to Segregation. Since both were scheduled to be transferred to the penitentiary the following day, they were simply locked in their cells.

A second event occurred at 3:00 p.m. when inmate Van Veelan, a "heavy" from the South Wing, got into a heated argument with Officer Lettall, who refused to let the prisoner out for a visit. While Van Veelan yelled at the guard, others in the Wing joined in. They began what one guard described as a "rumble." The prisoners stamped their feet, yelled, and banged their cell doors. The entire building trembled from their pounding. Extra staff were brought into the Unit, and the noise ended shortly after. At 3:20 p.m. all West Wing visits were cancelled.

The West Wing afternoon shift consisted of eight line guards and one Principal Officer. Given the explosive situation, staff were instructed to serve dinner, one tier at a time, and to ensure that all inmates from one tier were locked up before the next tier was served. Thus, if a problem developed, they would have to deal with twenty men at most. Dinner was served without incident; however, the lengthy process meant that officers missed their own meal break.

After the meal trays had been collected, prisoners were released from their cells and allowed to freely move about on their tiers. This was normal routine. However at 7:20 p.m., routine changed to rebellion when, on the left side of the fourth tier, several convicts set fire to a cell. As black smoke filled the left side of the Unit, five officers assembled on the fourth landing and prepared to fight the fire. Around them, they could hear plumbing being smashed and furnishings broken. Three guards attempted to keep the prisoners back, while the other two extinguished the fire. Another staff member tried to open the windows on the left side to allow the acrid smoke to vent. As he went onto the cat-walk to open the windows, inmates hurled jagged pieces of ceramic at him. He was ordered off for his own safety. After this, pandemonium broke loose on tier 4-Left, where the five officers were:

> During this time inmates were yelling "grab a guard." Staff were then ordered to leave the tier and secure the landing door, at which time fire hoses were deployed to drive the inmates back when they approached the front tier doors. There was also an attempt to use firehoses on the fire emergency doors at the end of tier 3-Left and tier 4-Right [by standing on the cat-walks]

141

to impede attacks on those doors. By this time the top three tiers on both sides were active with inmates smashing and hurling objects at staff and shouting obscenities. Additional fires also broke out on tier 4-Right and tier 5-Right.[21]

Staff reinforcements arrived a short time later. They stationed themselves on all five landings, deploying the fire hoses to prevent prisoners from rushing the endgates and erecting barricades.

At approximately 7:30 p.m. the Burnaby Fire Department arrived with additional hoses and high pressure nozzles. However, they declined to use the equipment on the inmates. Shortly afterwards, Burnaby RCMP officers arrived; they provided security around the West Wing in case of an escape attempt.

Just before 8:00 p.m., Local Director Hofseth arrived at the

Cells were demolished and set ablaze during November 1983, West Wing Riot.

institution and was briefed. He attempted to discover what the demands of the inmates were and called for a spokesman. No one came forward, and no demands were made. By all accounts, it appears that inmates were solely concerned with the destruction of the gaol.

It soon became apparent that inmates on the four tiers on the bottom two levels — remand inmates from the South Wing — wanted no part in the disturbance. Most of them were just milling about watching the violent activity above them. Although officials recognized that they didn't want to become involved, the guards waited until they had sufficient reinforcements before attempting to remove them. An hour later, fifty inmates from three of these tiers were removed; however, fourteen prisoners from tier 1-Left demanded to stay on the tier to show support for the others and agreed to be locked in their cells. There were still at least 100 rioters actively involved in the demolition of the West Wing.

The first goal of the destructive group was to cut through the wire mesh that extended along the walkways on each tier. Once this was accomplished they had access to the entire West Wing. Some of them jumped onto the roof of a small room at the end of tier 2-Right. They tore off wooden planks and made a bridgeway to the cat-walks. Although staff poured jets of water on them, they could not prevent them from gaining access. Once on the cat-walks, they sent all the televisions crashing to the floor. From this good vantage point, they threw porcelain shards and chunks of metal (torn from cell-door latches) at staff, after which they smashed most of the windows on the north side of the Wing.

Other prisoners tore the metal bed frames from their cell walls and used them as battering rams on the newly installed fire doors at the rear of each tier. Staff had initially prevented them from converging on the rear doors, by showering them from the catwalks, but were forced to retreat once the inmates gained access to them. With continual pounding these doors eventually buckled and gave way. The rioters now had access to the emergency rear stairwells, which were completely inaccessible to the staff. Bashing away at the rest of the emergency exits, they soon had access to both sides of the top three tiers. The prisoners "now represented a large rioting force, armed with metal bed legs, pieces of pipe and other objects."[22]

At 10:00 p.m. the rioters, who now had complete control of the Wing, attempted to breach the prison by chopping through the rear wall in the stairwell of the third landing. Layer by layer the old red brick and mortar began to crumble as they pounded away at the wall with their pipes. Within minutes all five courses of brick had been smashed through, and a man-sized hole opened up into the night. On the road below, police and corrections officers armed with rifles, shotguns, and fire hoses, were stationed ready to prevent any escape attempt. Some of the other prisoners had moved down to the right side of the second landing and attempted to break down the door that led to the West Wing exercise yard. The door took a considerable amount of abuse, but it held firm.

At 10:25 p.m. the fourteen inmates on tier 1-Left, who had earlier agreed to be locked up, were peacefully removed and locked in the East Wing.

At 10:30 p.m. a thirty-two man RCMP Emergency Response Team entered the prison grounds, marched down to the front entrance of the gaol, and stood by to await instructions. The rioters were then given a warning that if they did not surrender peacefully within the next thirty minutes, tear gas would be deployed and the tactical unit would begin removing them.

Eight minutes later, a small group of inmates approached the endgates and gave themselves up. By midnight the tactical team was no longer required. Prisoners began to file out in a peaceful line, cold, soaked, and tired. The last group to leave set a fire in the stairwell in a final act of defiance. This was quickly extinguished by the Fire Department, which had just moved in to assist with clean-up efforts.

By 1:40 a.m. all prisoners had been removed, searched, and transported to the East Wing and the Old Isolation Unit. Only six of the rioters were fortunate enough to be placed in the East Wing; the remaining eighty were crammed into the small underground facility. Some of the prisoners later complained that they had to run a gauntlet of baton-wielding guards as they were escorted down the stairs to the Old Segregation Unit. Medical officials examined all of them when they were first admitted, and again two days later. Many of them had cuts, minor sprains, and bruises — all injuries consistent with throwing sharp objects, smashing windows, and attempting to smash toilets and sinks with their feet. None of the injuries appeared to be related to beatings.

The following morning the media was given an opportunity to survey the damage to the riot-torn Wing. They discovered seventy-nine destroyed toilets, forty broken sinks, most of the windows shattered, numerous burned and water-damaged mattresses, and personal belongings in the majority of cells was lost. In addition, there was major structural damage to the West Wing. Many cell gates would require extensive repairs, six fire exit doors had been torn from their hinges, and there was a large hole in the prison wall. Damage was assessed at over $150,000, more than double the cost of any previous riot.

In the aftermath, the Inspection and Standards Division of the

Aftermath of the West Wing disturbance.

Corrections Branch reported on a serious security flaw in the newly installed fire doors, the breach of which had created enormous problems in containing and suppressing the riot:

> These doors were easily breached because of their tendency to buckle both horizontally and vertically. The welding, quality of attachment fixtures, and the technique itself of affixing the frame to the existing cement walls were inadequate. The method of installation was in accordance with the architect's specification, therefore, the contractor cannot be faulted on the installation method followed. The doors were installed where the original exits were cemented up for security reasons in 1930.[23]

The probable cause of the incident was a collaboration between the two groups of inmates to return to their respective Wings. The riot might not have occurred if the Warden and staff management had heeded warnings about placing these two groups together. Following the rampage, the West Wing was closed. It was only re-opened several years later to act as a temporary facility for inmates serving intermittent sentences on weekends. The South Wing returned to operation as a remand unit and the East Wing continued to house sentenced offenders.

Christmas "Gifts" for Two

The Christmas season was always depressing in Oakalla. Neither the inmates nor the staff wanted to be there and tensions often led to disturbances and other altercations. For this reason, December was always a prime month for escapes.

On Christmas Day 1986, two inmates took advantage of a loophole in security. It was near dinnertime and the two prisoners, along with several others, were responsible for hauling meal trays from the Kitchen to the East Wing via a tunnel between the two buildings. Several heavy iron gates in the tunnel separated the two units. The convicts noticed that the gate to the Kitchen had been left open to allow the carts of trays to be pushed into the tunnel. At the same time, the gate into the tunnel from the East Wing was opened by a staff member who went to pick up the meals.

The pair immediately ran from the East Wing, through the tunnel and into the Kitchen, where they passed several startled Kitchen employees.[24] Running out the unlocked rear door, they continued south, escaping over the perimeter fence. The two were not recaptured for some time.

Several months after this escape, after serving Oakalla for more than a dozen years, in which he had endured three major riots, years of economic restraint, and a sex scandal, Henry Bjarnason retired. When the popular warden took over the post, Corrections officials believed that he would be Oakalla's last warden. Although Bjarnason saw the opening of the VPSC in Vancouver, plans for other replacement facilities were delayed or suspended. When he passed the torch to the new warden, parts of the prison were still overcrowded, the Main Gaol was in a dilapidated state, and most prisoners in the East and South Wings spent much of their time on the narrow tiers without any activities, growing restless once again.

Eight

The New Year's Day Escape
1987-1990

Rene Aristide Gobillot began his career at Oakalla in May 1964 and left the prison several years later, as he worked his way up the promotional system. Returning on March 26, 1987, as the Centre's new district director (warden), he was almost immediately presented with his first disturbance.

On April 19, a tier of Westgate "B" inmates attempted to start a major disturbance after night lock-up by banging their cell walls and shouting threats. They did little damage to property, but their thunderous noise disrupted the entire unit. There had been other problems during the previous week, and the entire Segregation Unit, in Westgate "A," was full. The Night Gaoler contacted Gobillot, who gave permission to open the Old Segregation Unit and transfer the unruly group there.

The cells beneath the Cow Barns had not been used since the last major disturbance in November 1983. The twenty-one prisoners arrived to find the cells damp and dirty, and no mattresses or blankets. This particular Easter holiday was unseasonably cold. When Gobillot inspected the unit at 8:30 a.m. the following morning, some of the

Typical cell in Westgate.

offenders were shivering in their cells. The steam heat that filtered through the prison by old piping had not yet reached them. He decided to keep the unit supplied and clean in the event further incidents warranted its use.

Dummies Fool Guards
Westgate was originally designed for workshops. However, in order

to relieve over-crowding it was converted in the 1950s into a "temporary facility." The exterior walls were constructed by overlapping layers of wooden planks, then finished with corrugated iron siding. Prisoners had little difficulty in burrowing through them and escaping. On December 11, 1987, three convicts from a protective custody tier escaped during a recreation period. Guards made several trips up and down the tier during this time, but the escapees concealed themselves by lying between the top of the far-end cell and the ceiling, where they pried away at the wooden wall. When a formal count was made, the officer mistakenly counted three dummies of stuffed cloth that were "sleeping" in the escapees' beds. Within hours, the convicts had pried open the outer layer of corrugated siding and escaped over a nearby fence. They were considered medium security-risk, and the public was not informed of the escape. Two weeks later, however, the outside world would be well aware of turmoil within Oakalla.

1987 Riot and New Year's Day Escape
The mass escape of thirteen maximum-security prisoners from the Old Segregation Unit is considered perhaps the most vivid event in the prison's violent history. The escape even attracted international media attention. Stirring television interviews were given by guards, with disguised faces and voices, who described horrendous working conditions and provided the "true story" behind the escape. Even more sensational was a clandestine television interview with one of the escaped convicts, while he was still on the run. Allegations of improprieties, and public concern over the affair, quickly led the government to launch a full inquiry to investigate just how these prisoners managed to escape, and who was to blame.

Several days before Christmas, several guards had heard that some South Wing prisoners, who were looking at lengthy penitentiary sentences, were planning to escape, and were offering up to $1500 cash to anyone who would assist them.

Christmas Day, 1987
A Christmas service was held in the Chapel, on the top floor of the Main Gaol. Following prison policy, inmates from the various units sat separate from one another. After the Friday service, inmate Hoy, from the South Wing, shook the hand of an East Wing convict. Believing that contraband had been passed, officers apprehended the two men and frisked them, but found nothing.

149

Boxing Day, 1987

On weekends at Oakalla, if prisoners filled out a request form, they could watch late-night television. The South Wing filled out such a request during Boxing Day — a Saturday. However, when the night shift officers came on duty, the request had not been forwarded, and the television sets were turned off. The inmates yelled in protest, one of them set a small fire, and the sets were turned back on.

December 27, 1987

During breakfast hours, one of the South Wing inmates passed a guard a note that stated there was going to be an escape attempt through the fire door on tier 1-Right. Officers found that a lock on that door had indeed been tampered with. It was decided that, until other arrangements could be made, prisoners on that tier would be locked in their cells.

Being a Sunday, there was once again a church service, and, on this occasion, an unusually large number of inmates placed their names on the list to attend. At least four of them were believed to be key players in the planned escape attempt. According to testimony in the subsequent Inquiry, inmate Dean, whose name was on the list, was believed to have been the central figure. Staff in the Wing thought these prisoners might attempt to take hostages during the service, as there was usually just one officer there from each Wing. Rather than cancelling the service for the South Wing, which might start a disturbance, they decided to send an additional escorting officer. One of the South Wing guards, Officer P. Kitto, who was a conscientious officer with more than eight years' experience, enforced the prison rules by the letter. At the same time there were other junior officers in the Wing who, for various reasons, were more lax in enforcing regulations. For this reason, Kitto was not well liked by some South Wing inmates.

During the service, Kitto and the other South Wing officer decided that they would strictly enforce the rule of no communication between the units. Below, Officer Kitto gives his version of events during the service:

> Dean positioned himself near a post and then another individual from the East Wing also positioned himself near the post. Now prior to that they had not been able to communicate too well their plans that we suspected they were going to take hostages... I positioned myself

150

behind Dean so that they could be aware that I was there and keep communication down to a minimum. There were some hand signals going back and forth, some gesturing, and they were trying to communicate. I motioned to Dean to stop at which point he became enraged. He stood up and threw his book to the floor and started yelling at me. I said, 'We had better take you out of here, lets go back to the unit.'[1]

Dean was then taken out of the chapel, handcuffed with his hands behind his back, and escorted downstairs to the South Wing entrance. On the way down, Dean complained about being escorted with handcuffs on, and was verbally abusive towards Kitto.

When I got down to One Level I undid the handcuffs and as I was reaching to put them away, Dean spun around and struck me across the head. I tried to re-restrain him and I wasn't getting anywhere because he's a pretty tough boy. Several officers came to my assistance and we still had a difficult time restraining him.[2]

Dean was tackled by the other guards, forced to the floor, and re-handcuffed. The guards were about to escort him to Segregation, however, they had to wait several minutes while a group of protective custody prisoners filed slowly through Centre Hall. During the scuffle Dean's forehead was deeply lacerated above one eye and the gash began to bleed profusely. At that moment, inmate Hoy, who had also left the church service, came down the stairs and saw Dean standing there handcuffed, with his face covered in blood. Hoy ran back up the stairs, yelling to the others that the guards had just beaten Dean while he was handcuffed. Hoy was quickly restrained and locked in an empty cell on tier 1-Right, but the damage had been done.

Reaction to the alleged beating was fierce. The only tier locked up at the time was 1-Right, while the remaining prisoners were free to roam. They began to shout threats and bang on their cell bars. Most of the staff on duty were inexperienced, some not knowing even how to operate tier locking mechanisms. Principal Officer Sahota ordered the guards to lock down the South Wing. The first tier they approached was 2-Left, which housed the South Wing cleaners, who were rarely locked in their cells, and were the Wing's "heavies." When the handful of young officers walked onto the tier they were met with a show of force. Several of the larger inmates approached the guards and told them there was no way they were going to lock-up. A muscular prisoner, with tattoos around his neck, angrily shouted: "If we lock up now, we lose. You wanna lock us up, you better bring in the f——ing army!" For the moment the guards backed down and waited for reinforcements from other units.

While the officers stood there waiting, inmates on tiers 1-Right and 2-Right began to smash the furniture and plumbing in their cells. A sink smashed violently against an endgate as they tried to ram it off its hinges. On 2-Right inmates brandished a hunting knife and a machete. Several prisoners broke mop handles and fashioned them into crude spears to throw at the guards as they crossed in front of an endgate. Fires were set at the far ends of the tiers; before the official word came to deploy the fire hoses, officers attempted to douse the flames using portable extinguishers. As one guard ventured onto 1-Right to douse the fire, a prisoner locked in the first cell threw a cup of urine in his face.

When the uprising began, Warden Gobillot and the South Wing's Senior Correctional Officer, G. Craig were contacted at their homes. When they arrived they met with inmate Dzvonik, who also called upon inmate Dean, to hear the demands of the inmates. Dean was advised that his alleged assault by Officer Kitto was being investigated by the RCMP. To bring an end to the fracas, both parties agreed to the following terms:

(a) Kitto and the other officers involved in the altercation would be kept out of the unit temporarily;
(b) the inmates on tier 1R would be released from their cells;
(c) the mess created on the tiers would be cleaned up by the inmates; and
(d) Dean would be returned to the unit while the RCMP investigated his charges against Officer Kitto.[3]

The parties also agreed that there would be a search of the Unit in the afternoon, while the prisoners were out at "yard." Sahota was ordered to organize the search, but was unable to round up enough officers to conduct one. When Craig returned to the South Wing after the yard period, he was dismayed to discover that the search had not been carried out. Craig then ordered members of the afternoon shift to conduct one. This was not a full lock-down search, and it was suspended during the dinner hour.

During the search, Officer Reilly intercepted an envelope containing drugs that was dropped from inmate McKay on 4-Right for Dean

Tier 1-Right, maximum-security South Wing.

on tier 1. When Reilly picked up the contraband, the prisoner threatened the officer's life. At about the same time, inmate Hall was brought out of his cell so it could be searched. Hall yelled and threatened staff, punched his cell door — and broke his left hand. None of the weapons seen earlier were recovered during the search, and a number of the guards, Craig included, felt that it was not conducted effectively and was more a show of authority.

December 28, 1987
By the time the afternoon shift arrived, the South Wing had become extremely volatile. The inmate who had threatened Officer Reilly the night before had now been charged with the offence; when the guard came on duty, the prisoners began to abuse him and other officers verbally. Some chanted the guards' names, threatening

them. Others shouted: "You're going to see blood" and "We're going to break this place up!"[4]

The officers on duty became afraid for their own safety as well as the security of the unit. Reilly contacted Officer L. Buss, a union shop steward, who was working in another unit. He in turn spoke to an acting deputy director and advised him of the explosive situation. Contacted at home, Craig returned to Oakalla. After a discussion with staff, and a tour of the Wing, he decided that another thorough search should be undertaken.

During these discussions, the inmates were locked down for dinner. However, by the time another search was initiated it was after 6:00 p.m. and several of them were banging on their cell doors, demanding to be released. Craig went to the tiers, told the prisoners that he had authorized another frisk, and that, on this occasion, it would be full lock-down. This news was met with further hostility; to some inmates, Craig's actions breached the agreement that had been reached the day before.

Two search teams were deployed, one on tier 4-Left and the other on 1-Right. In the first cell of 1-Right officers recovered two sharpened brass rods, hidden in the mattress. When the inmate was informed that he would be charged, other prisoners shouted that the guards had planted the weapons in his cell.

Inmate Dzvonik was in the second cell on 4-Left. He was brought out, taken onto the fourth landing, and told to remove his clothes. Irate at having to be skin-frisked, he picked up a metal garbage can and threw it, narrowly missing a guard. Several officers subdued him, but the scuffle had created a great deal of noise, and some of the prisoners shouted that Dzvonik was being beaten. Since he had been their negotiator, this had an explosive effect, and "all hell broke loose."

In what was described as "utter bedlam," prisoners began to destroy their cells, break furniture, and set it on fire. Many of them booted their toilets and sinks to pieces. The search was abandoned and officers were instructed to deploy fire hoses. Protecting themselves with shields, guards walked along the catwalks and saturated the more violent inmates. A number of prisoners later complained that they were injured by flying debris from the high-pressure hoses, and it was the streams of water, and not they, which had destroyed the cell fixtures.

As nearly twenty fires burned within the confines of the wing, black smoke began to billow and Craig had the windows opened. The electric heaters were also turned off to prevent the possibility of electrical shock as hundreds of gallons of water cascaded from the tiers. By 9:30 p.m. every inmate in the South Wing was subdued and stood shivering in his drenched cell. Almost every cell had been destroyed, and damage was estimated at more than $100,000.

The violence, however, had not yet come to an end. The whole institution had been shaking for almost three hours and the 150 inmates in the East Wing were highly agitated. The bottom two tiers refused to lock-up at 10:00 p.m. and prisoners began to erect barricades at the endgates with overturned tables and benches. This time the administration was not caught off-guard. The tactical team was assembled and waiting in Centre Hall. When it stormed the Wing, the convicts dispersed and ran for their cells. Nineteen of the instigators were taken from their cells and booked into the Westgate Segregation Unit, which was now virtually full.

This riot was the only major disturbance at Oakalla where the warden did not personally attend to take control. Although Gobillot had been contacted at his residence at 6:30 p.m., he decided that the situation was in capable hands.

December 29, 1987
Early the next morning Gobillot met with Craig and Deputy District Director Grant Stevens. The men decided to move the South Wing prisoners to the vacant West Wing, except for those who were considered the instigators. It was felt that they might incite another riot in the West Wing if given the opportunity. The Segregation Unit was full, so Gobillot received permission from the Deputy Commissioner of Corrections to reopen the Old Segregation Unit (O.S.U.) and assigned Deputy Director Stevens to oversee this move and the inmate "extraction process."

This process of "extracting" prisoners from their cells involved two officers, carrying shields, who would approach the front of each cell, followed by three officers who would enter the cell and take the prisoner into custody. As further protection, two of the entering officers carried batons, and the third held a mace canister. When they arrived at a cell, one of the guards would instruct the inmate what to do, and the consequences of failing to comply. The inmate would then be handcuffed and taken off the tier. Craig had compiled a list of fourteen of the most troublesome prisoners in his unit, which he passed on to the leader of the cell extraction team. If the prisoner had been compliant and his name was not on the list he was taken to the West Wing. The others were booked in the O.S.U. Of the fifty-six men in the Wing, a dozen violently resisted and were hit in the legs with batons and sprayed with mace.

There were wide-spread reports in the media that several prisoners had been severely beaten by guards. Most were unfounded. One story was that an inmate had been struck with a baton in the testicles and they had swollen to the size of grapefruits. It was later confirmed that this injury was self-inflicted. Another prisoner slashed his wrists with a shard of broken porcelain and, in his own blood, wrote "Helter Skelter" on his cell wall.

By the time the transfer process was completed, thirty-four prisoners were sent to the West Wing and twenty-two went to the O.S.U. (fourteen from Craig's list and another eight who had been difficult during the cell extractions). Most of the prisoners in the O.S.U. were placed in regular punishment cells, however, others were placed in "Quiet Cells" at the rear. Seven were subsequently removed from the O.S.U. and taken to the Health Care Centre for medical treatment.

Since the O.S.U. had not been in full operation for several years, few officers were familiar with its operational procedures, or even how some of the locking mechanisms worked. Several Quiet Cells had

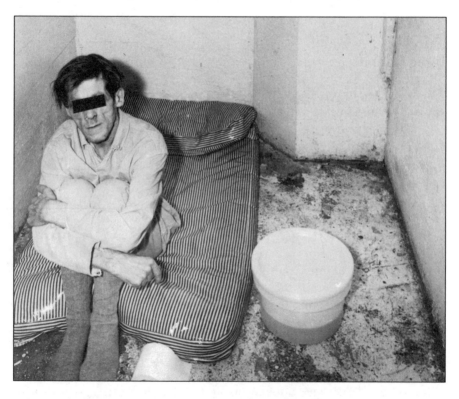

Dungeon-like cells of the Old Segregation Unit.

156

locking devices that were like no others at Oakalla. No keys were required to operate their inner doors; instead, a lever arm, projecting from the door, was lowered to release the locks. A pin could be inserted beneath this lever, which would prevent it from being lowered. However, each of these cells were equipped with an outer wooden security door, which could be locked with a key.

December 30, 1987

The operation of the Unit was originally placed in the hands of Principal Officer Bevans, who operated the O.S.U. as a regular Segregation facility. But Bevans left for holidays on December 30, and his replacement was unfamiliar with standard operating procedures. Matters were further muddled when Gobillot toured the O.S.U. and advised the guards to "run the unit, so far as possible, as if it were a regular unit."[5] He also approved the issuing of tobacco products to the prisoners, which was contrary to unit policy. Later, they were also provided with toiletries, such as disposable razors and toothbrushes.

As a result of Gobillot's directive, officers working the afternoon shift decided to leave the outer wooden doors open on all the Quiet Cells, as it was colder and darker back there. They were never shut again.

December 31, 1987

In the early afternoon Deputy Director Stevens inspected the O.S.U. At the subsequent Inquiry he testified that he found the place in an "untidy" condition, but that he never noticed the wooden doors to the Quiet Cells were open. Commissioner Drost replied, "I find it difficult to understand how Stevens, who testified that it was his expectation that the wooden doors would be kept closed and locked, could have overlooked the fact that they were open at the time of his inspection."[6]

It appeared that the concerns of management were primarily for inmate comfort, so as not to cause further unrest, and the safety and security of the Unit came a distant second. As Commissioner Drost explained, "It seems that senior management believed that the O.S.U. was a very secure unit simply because no one had ever escaped from it."[7] Drost was mistaken: on July 31, 1962, five dangerous convicts had escaped from beneath the Cow Barns. Any lessons that might have been learned from the previous escape had clearly eroded with the passing of time. The O.S.U. was actually Oakalla's least secure unit. In every other unit, if an inmate managed to free himself from his cell, he still had to pass through an endgate before he could escape from the unit itself. Moreover, any guard on that tier would not have keys for the endgates or outer doors on him. In the O.S.U., there were no gates separating the officer's work area from the tier of cells, and the key to the outside door was kept with the officers inside the unit.

Yet another serious breach of prison policy had been overlooked. In every other unit that was separate from the Main Gaol, officers were required to carry personal alarm transmitters. This was especially the rule in the Segregation and Observation Units, where officers continuously worked with high-security-risk inmates. At the time, those prisoners in the O.S.U. were believed to be Oakalla's most dangerous, yet none of the officers was issued an emergency beeper. As if it were fate, even the portable two-way radio kept in the O.S.U. was out of order. The only means of communication was an old rotary-dial telephone.

At 10:55 p.m., Auxiliary Security Officer Bainas was the first to arrive at the O.S.U. to relieve the afternoon shift. According to prison policy, he should not have been assigned to a Segregation Unit before completing the basic training program. With just over six months' experience, this officer knew little about emergency procedures in the regular units — not to mention the O.S.U. When he arrived, he met with a staff member who quickly ran Bainas through the operation of the unit, had him confirm the head-count, and then handed him the keys. He was also instructed to leave the wooden doors of the Quiet Cells open, and that the inmates were allowed tobacco products, but no matches. If they wanted to smoke, he would have to go around and light their cigarettes.

At 11:00 p.m. Correctional Officer Fenton, with little more than two years' experience, entered the Unit. Although he had previously worked in the Westgate "A" Segregation Unit, he had never been to the O.S.U., and, as he later testified, "I did not even know who was in there or why."[8] When he arrived, the other officers left the two guards for the night.

These grave breaches of prison policy set the stage where a serious incident was, if not inevitable, at least predictable. The two officers performed their regular checks at 11:30 p.m. and at midnight, while the outside world celebrated the birth of a new year, all was deathly quiet beneath the Cow Barn.

New Year's, 1988
At 12:30 a.m. the two officers did another count. During their rounds various inmates asked them to get water, or light a smoke;

some even asked for coffee. A number of them kept asking about the time. The officers lied, saying it was before midnight, hoping the men would go to sleep, and not create a lot of noise by celebrating New Year's.

After making their rounds, Fenton and Bainas returned to the office at the front of the Unit and began thumbing through old newspapers and magazines. While they were settling in for a long and boring night, at the other end of the Unit, in one of the Quiet Cells, inmate McKay had just freed himself from his cell. Under cover of darkness he crossed the hallway over to inmate White's cell, where he removed the security pin and opened his door. How McKay was able to escape from his cell remains a mystery. The most plausible explanation was demonstrated by Grant Stevens during a media tour of the institution following the escape. "Deputy Director Grant Stevens showed how McKay reached beneath his Plexiglass cell door [the food tray slot] and used the weighted [with a bag of peanuts] sock to unhook the lock."[9] The sock was tied to a piece of torn bed sheet which was thrown over the door lever. When pulled down — providing the locking pin was not in place — the lever lowered and unlocked the door.

The Royal Commission offered three possible explanations why the pin may not have been properly seated:

(1) an officer, when returning the inmate to his cell, neglected to insert the pin and make sure the handle was in the locked position;

(2) the inmate himself may have discovered a means of disengaging the pin as well as pulling down the lever; or

(3) another inmate, during the course of ablutions or while assisting the staff by passing around coffee, entered the quiet cell area and disengaged the pin.

The third alternative seems to the most likely reason.[10]

At approx. 12:40 a.m. Officer Bainas heard a click coming from the rear of the Unit — the Quiet Cell area. His partner Fenton also heard it. Bainas wondered if maybe one of the prisoners was trying to commit suicide. He talked it over with his partner and they decided to do their 1:00 a.m. check early. The pair were walking past the regular cells when one inmate stopped them and asked for tobacco, Officer Fenton sent Bainas back to the office to get some. They walked a little further, and another inmate asked for a light, and once again Bainas went back and got a match. As they got near the Quiet Cell area, another prisoner asked for water. Officer Bainas turned around and walked back to the front of the Unit and fetched it. At the same time Officer Fenton walked into the Quiet Cell area and said, "Who wants it?" He turned around, and in the near-dark hallway, saw the outline of a man standing in a cell doorway. It was inmate White. Suddenly, from out of the shadows, inmate McKay came up behind Fenton and wrapped his arm around the guard's throat. With his other hand he held a crude knife — a razor blade melted into a toothbrush — to his neck.

By the time Bainas turned around with the jug of water, White was rushing towards him with a wooden toilet-bowl plunger in his hand. Bewildered, Bainas froze then tried to retreat and sound the alarm. Realizing that the only way he could call for help was to dial the phone, he stopped and prepared to fight. McKay then came out from the shadows holding his hostage. Bainas looked at Fenton and saw blood trickling from a small slit in his cheek. Bainas started to creep back to the office, but he was warned that, if he took another step, the guard was dead. Bainas wanted to call Control and then deal with the situation, but he knew that to do so might cost his partner's life. While he was struggling with the decision, Officer Fenton was pleading with Bainas to co-operate, and spare his life. One of the inmates then told Bainas to get down on his knees, and he decided to comply.

> I laid down and they threw a towel over my head and then there was chaos after that. They were running around and an inmate took the keys off me, went into the office... got a pair of handcuffs and handcuffed me [with my arms] behind the back. I could see [Officer Fenton] being tied up with a torn sheet. At first it was just the two of them, and then they started opening cells. That's when everybody started running around saying: 'Kill the pigs.' Some other inmates were saying: 'No. Leave the pigs alone, you're free...' I thought I was dead, the first thing I said to myself was, 'Jesus I hope being killed doesn't hurt much.'
> The towel then came off my face, and I had my glasses on. I looked up and I saw this big Indian, he's there staring down at me and I thought oh shit here it comes. I said, 'don't kick me in the face, I don't want to be blind. Please.' He took the glasses off and put them in my shirt pocket and then re-tied the towel over my head.[11]

The two officers were spared death or at least a brutal beating. The prisoners picked them up, dragged them into separate cells across from each other, and then locked them in. Some inmates continued to make death threats, and others kicked them saying, "How do you like this, pig?" There was a big scramble for their clothes, including their patrol jackets and personal clothing. One prisoner remained locked in his cell, wanting nothing to do with the incident; another decided not to go, although he was released. The remaining thirteen took the keys, unlocked the front door, and ran.

Once up the Cow Barn stairs, the escapees split into small groups and continued to flee south, past the Lakeside Centre for Women, and over the dilapidated fence in the south-east corner of the property. Coincidentally, Oakalla's only armed Prowl Officer, who might have had a chance to stop some of them, or at least sound the alarm, happened to be relieving officers in the Main Gaol for their lunch and coffee breaks. In a matter of minutes the desperadoes had just pulled off the second largest prison break in British Columbia's penal history. The thirteen maximum security escapees, all considered at the time to be armed and dangerous, were:

1. G. Dewhirst, 21, charged with first degree murder.
2. D. Fetter, 18, charged with break and enter.
3. G. Gravelle, 39, charged with armed robbery.
4. S. Gray, 23, charged with break and enter.
5. T. Hall, 23, sentenced to three years for robbery.
6. G. Hicik, 20, charged with robbery.
7. A. Isbister, 26, charged with robbery.
8. R. Janenicke, 28, charged with robbery.
9. D. Lee, 30, charged with robbery.
10. B. McKay, 32, charged with robbery.
11. D. Smith, 20, charged with robbery.
12. N. White, 22, sentenced to nine years for robbery.
13. R. Williams, 20, charged with break and enter.

The escape was not discovered until shortly after 1:00 a.m. Principal Officer Claassen was working in Central Control in the Main Gaol. After failing to receive the routine hourly report, at 1:05 a.m. he telephoned the O.S.U. On the first call he let the phone ring "five or six times." Minutes later he called back, and there was still no answer. Claassen then instructed a number of tactical team officers to go over to the O.S.U. and investigate.[12] A few minutes later one of the guards returned to the Main Gaol saying that the door to the O.S.U.

was wide open. He grabbed a sidearm, another officer took a shotgun, and they ran back to the stairway leading to the "Hole." They could hear calls for help coming from inside the unit, but they were unsure if they were genuine or some sort of "set-up" by the inmates. The guard carrying the shotgun decided to take matters into his own hands.

Inside the unit he found the two officers still bound and locked in separate cells. He immediately telephoned Central Control and informed Claassen of the escape. This officer showed no compassion towards his workmates; he told them they had better have a good explanation for what happened or they would be out of a job. He then left, and it was not until an RCMP member arrived some time later that the two guards were set free from the cells. They were still in shock, and Bainas had suffered nerve damage to his hands after having tight handcuffs on his wrists for more than three-quarters of an hour. Even so, Deputy Director Stevens directed them to write a detailed report on the occurrence, apparently showing little regard for their emotional or mental well-being.

The RCMP had been notified of the escape at 1:20 a.m. Oakalla officers grabbed shotguns and sidearms, jumped into prison vehicles, and headed off grounds in all directions. This was not a coordinated search, and targeted various locations on their own accord. Meanwhile, the RCMP were not having much luck due to the fifteen minute time-delay in being notified, and frosty weather conditions prevented their dogs from tracking a scent.

On the Lam

As residents of Burnaby celebrated the beginning of a new year, some of them met up with the fugitives. A young couple were about to leave a neighbourhood pub on nearby Kingsway. As they sat in their car waiting for it to warm up, they were approached by three escapees. One opened the passenger door and pulled the young woman out of her seat, while another tried to drag the driver out. Although the young man put up a fight, he was beaten in the face until the three were able to drag him from his car. As they got into the car and attempted to drive away, the owner jumped onto the hood and tried to open the door. The vehicle sped across the parking lot, with the man still hanging on, then the driver swerved erratically, throwing the owner to the ground. The fugitives side-swiped another car and then roared out onto Kingsway and sped away. Later that morning, the abandoned automobile was recovered by Surrey RCMP.

During the night and into New Year's Day, accused murderer

Dewhirst travelled nearly 100 kilometres from Oakalla to the quiet farming community of Chilliwack. In the early afternoon, several police officers surrounded the prisoner's parents' home and took him back into custody.

Three of the fugitives — Fetter, Smith, and Isbister — spent a day together and on New Year's night they went drinking in a New Westminster pub. As the men sat at a table talking with a young woman, police were tipped-off as to their location and apprehended them there.

On January 2, escapee Hall contacted a local television station through an "intermediary" and agreed to an exclusive interview with BCTV news reporter Alyn Edwards. The two men met at an undisclosed location and recorded the interview. Hall blamed the guards for the riot, alleging excessive force and brutality. He claimed that he escaped from Oakalla because he needed "a break" from its oppressive conditions. Below is a portion of the taped interview, which was later broadcast on the evening news:

> Hall: "The next thing I know is, some drunk guards were pulling out fire hoses and hosing people down."
> Edwards: "How do you know the guards were drunk, were they obviously intoxicated?"
> Hall: "Oh there was guards stumbling around, falling against walls, and you could smell it, the booze right on them."
> Edwards: "Is that a regular occurrence?"
> Hall: "Maybe because of the holidays, I don't know."
> (Later)
> Edwards: "How long were the prisoners hosed down?"
> Hall: "Well, speaking for myself, and I have witnesses, they were at my cell, hosing me down, anywhere from seven to ten minutes."[13]

Following the interview, the reporter allowed the escapee to leave without making any attempt to have him apprehended. The Attorney-General initially contemplated laying criminal charges against the reporter, saying that Edwards had "stooped to a new low in journalism." Edwards, however, argued that Hall had given him his word that he would surrender in a few days, once he got his "head together." On January 5, Hall did indeed turned himself in.

During the riot, the prisoners had made up "Death Lists" which bore the names of four to six officers. Inmates had eerily chanted their names, hollering threats against them. At the time of the riot these threats were taken seriously; however, there were more urgent matters to deal with. Now that some of these prisoners were loose in the community, with access to weapons, several of the officers feared for their lives. One guard on the list locked himself in his home and kept a loaded shotgun, rifle, and handgun nearby. Officer Kitto's name had been at the top of both lists, underlined, and highlighted. He asked the Corrections Branch for permission to carry a sidearm, but was denied. He then contacted the RCMP, who took the threats seriously enough to move him and his family into a Burnaby motel. A few days later, an escapee whom Kitto had known for some time was recaptured. Kitto interviewed him and discussed the likelihood of the other escapees attempting to carry out their threats. The prisoner told him that he had been in contact with a number of the other escapees and that they were now only interested in avoiding apprehension. With that reassurance, and the fact that there had been no further threats, Kitto and his family returned to their home and the other officers breathed a little easier.

On January 4, inmate Gray was arrested when he was found hiding in a closet in a relative's apartment in Burnaby. Later that evening, Delta police officers apprehended fugitives White and McKay at a home on Scott Road. White attempted to flee, but the officers quickly caught up with him and took him into custody.

Inmate Hicik, who had spent most of his time holed up in a friend's Burnaby apartment, "boozing and phoning girls," was contacted by police on January 7 and told that his place was surrounded. He gave up, without incident. In the weeks that followed, the remaining four escapees were all eventually seized by the police and charged with escaping lawful custody.

Officer Bound and Gagged

Several weeks after the mass escape, South Wing inmate trusties, now housed in the West Wing, were employed to help remove the tons of broken debris left by the riot. On February 7, 1988, three prisoners, working under the supervision of a guard, continued the clean-up effort. After a short time, two of them jumped the officer, gagged his mouth with a cloth and tied his wrists behind his back. They then did the same to the third inmate, fearing he would "rat" to the staff. The prisoners then cut a lock off a fire exit door, scaled several fences, and quickly escaped. These prisoners were considered maximum security; one had been remanded on a murder charge.

In 1988 escapes were virtually eliminated when guard-dog patrols were introduced.

The Inquiry

In response to public concern for the overall security of Oakalla, and numerous allegations of improprieties reported by inmates, guards, and management, the provincial government launched a Royal Commission of Inquiry on January 6. Vancouver County Court Judge Ian Drost was appointed Commissioner. The hearings began on January 29, and continued until the end of May. During that time more than fifty witnesses were called before the Commission to testify. In late 1988, the Commissioner's findings were published in a 125-page report.

The report noted five specific "causes" of the escape:

1. Management's failure to recognize the insecurity of the O.S.U.;
2. Confusion over lack of instructions on how to operate the O.S.U.;
3. Leaving the unit improperly staffed, and not instructing officers on how to use the unique locking device;
4. Failure to provide guards in the O.S.U. with personal

alarm transmitters; and
5. A lack of vigilance on the part of some of the officers who worked in the unit.[14]

In the report, Commissioner Drost also dismissed allegations of drunkenness and brutality on the part of the guards. The Commissioner's final recommendation was to proceed with the establishment of new institutions and "close the doors of Oakalla forever."

Aftermath

Early in 1988, initiatives were undertaken to reduce the number of escapes. Plans for the phasing-out of Oakalla were well underway, and the high cost of installing new security systems could not be justified. Officials decided on adding guard dogs, escorted by armed handlers, to patrol the inside perimeter of the institution. The result was a dramatic reduction in escapes. During the remainder of 1988 there was only one escape, by two inmates from a minimum-security work gang. In 1989 there were none. This was a first in more than fifty years! Ironically, a relatively inexpensive solution to a problem that had plagued Oakalla for so many decades, was discovered only in its final years.

In 1989, inmates McKay and White were convicted of kidnapping, prison breach, and assault with a weapon, for the hostage-taking of the two officers beneath the Cow Barn. They each received additional five-year sentences.

Officer Bainas returned to work after recovering from his physical injuries and continued his service at Oakalla. He later transferred to the new Fraser Regional Correctional Centre. Officer Fenton was on disability for a longer period. He did return to the Corrections Branch for a time, but eventually left the service.

Officer Kitto, who went through a difficult time following the crisis, learned that prison guards who have been through similar circumstances often encounter what are commonly referred to as "post-traumatic stress disorders." Over a two-year period he successfully initiated a Critical Incident Response Team for the Corrections Branch, to assist officers who had been through a work-related crisis.

In early 1990, Warden Gobillot left Oakalla to oversee the construction and completion of one of the prison's replacement facilities, the Fraser Regional Correctional Centre. Deputy Director Stevens then assumed Gobillot's position, his mandate being to ensure the closure of Oakalla.

Nine

Oakalla Closes
1990-1991

By the time Grant Stevens took over, the prison was well on its way to closing. The provincial government had pledged that Oakalla would be gone by 1986; however, economic restraint forced the closing date ahead each passing year. Frustration over unfulfilled promises to replace the Centre had manifested itself in numerous riots and disturbances. In 1987 the Corrections Branch finally established the locations for a new facility for sentenced male offenders, a new remand centre, and an institution for female prisoners. But it would be several more years before the new prisons could be inhabited, and, at Oakalla, hostilities continued.

The final major disturbance occurred late in the evening on April 17, 1990. A group of South Wing inmates began demanding that a prisoner be returned to his cell after he had been removed and sent to Segregation for assaulting an officer. When officials rejected their demand, some prisoners smashed property and lit fires, and many more — forty-six of them — destroyed toilets, television sets, and windows. Once again, fire hoses were turned on to quell the fracas. By 3:00 a.m. the prisoners had been moved by the tactical team to the vacant

West Wing. Those deemed to be instigators were transferred to the Segregation Unit, and some of them later faced criminal charges.

The Replacement Centres

Clearing the land for Maple Ridge's Fraser Regional Correctional Centre began in 1986 with the assistance of inmates from nearby Pine Ridge Camp. The engineering company, Phillips Barratt, designed the 254-bed Centre, while the main contractor was Farmer Construction Ltd. At a cost of $47.3 million, the facility was ready for occupancy on July 3, 1990. When it opened, Oakalla inmates from Westgate and the Health Care Centre were transferred there.

The Burnaby Correctional Centre for Women opened on April 2, 1991, replacing the Lakeside Correctional Centre. The 140-bed prison on the south flats of Burnaby, near the Fraser River, houses provincial offenders, and up to fifty women serving federal sentences.

Vancouver architect Zoltan Kiss designed the 150-bed Surrey Pretrial Services Centre, while Stuart Olson Construction Inc. was awarded the contract to build this $40.5 million high-tech Remand Centre. It officially opened May 6, 1991.

These new facilities are modern in every way. Both the inmates and staff are constantly monitored by hundreds of closed-circuit television cameras, which are mounted throughout the interior and exterior of the prison. Guards no longer have brass keys, but coded credit-card-sized passes. There are no longer armed guards in towers, prowl officers, or guard-dogs watching the prison grounds. Surveillance cameras and motion detectors now monitor the perimeter.

Inside, bullet-proof glass has replaced iron bars. Each floor of every wing is completely sealed off from the next, creating a quieter living environment than the old Main Gaol. The constant banging of cell doors and shouts of men no longer echo throughout the units. If there were a disturbance on one tier, the rest of the prison's inmates would probably be totally oblivious to it.

The units are all painted a calming pastel pink or blue, the ranges are wide and open, and inmates are locked up at night in what look more like small hotel rooms than prison cells. Guards work in "living units" which are equipped with microwave ovens, fridges, pool tables, and wall-to-wall carpeting. Many citizens have complained that the offenders have far superior living conditions in the new prisons than what they will have once released into the community. Then Solicitor-General Russ Fraser responded by saying: "It may look luxurious, but the fact is, you're still locked in."[1] While people may argue that pleasant living arrangements have no punitive or deterrent effect on these criminals, some former Oakalla guards favour them because they have found less hostility and outbreaks of violence in this new environment. A common saying around Oakalla was that inmates were only in prison for a short time, while guards were doing life on the installment plan. Many of these officers appreciate working in a healthier prison.

The Final Year

For those — and there were many — who believed that Oakalla would go out with a bang, the necessary elements for one massive and destructive riot certainly existed. When the new prison in Maple Ridge opened in the summer of 1990, inmates from the Westgate and Hospital Units who were not sent to the new Centre were transferred to the Main Gaol. Transfers of entire units have historically brought disruptions; in this instance prisoners were furious because they had been moved from their spacious units to the narrow confines of the South and West Wings. Their anger boiled over on the evening of May 20, 1991, when nearly all of the 122 West Wing inmates began to yell and rattle their bars. Although some property was damaged during the two-hour uprising, it was not the all-out rampage that everyone had feared. The tactical team was quickly assembled and ushered ten of the most unruly prisoners to Segregation.

What might have been the final big break from Oakalla never occurred — thanks to a little bit of luck. Only several months before it closed, a young officer in Central Control at the Main Gaol was enquiring how the telephone monitoring system for "glass visits" worked. There were visitors in Centre Hall at the time, talking to prisoners over the special two-way phones. The guard randomly decided to listen in on a conversation between a West Wing inmate and his "girlfriend." He heard the prisoner tell the woman that the "big break-out" would be going down that night, and that he would be seeing her shortly. A few hours later, the West Wing was locked-down and guards began to search for cut bars or jimmied doors. After a thorough frisk, they had still found nothing. Then, just as they were about to leave, an officer noticed a piece of cardboard up against the outer wall on tier 2-Right. When he lifted it he discovered that all the bricks had been removed, except for one course which was loosely fitted into place to cover the hole from the outside. On closer inspection of the West Wing, officers also found that wire mesh leading to the tiers above had been cut, which meant that inmates from the upper tiers could have climbed down to the opening on tier-2. A man-sized hole had also been dug under a perimeter fence on the south side of Oakalla. Had the plan not been discovered, potentially half of the 150 maximum-security prisoners could have escaped.

Oakalla Closes

The last prisoners at Oakalla were all remand inmates, waiting for the Surrey Pretrial Centre to open. On June 29, Sheriffs' vans transferred half of them to the new Centre, and on the last day of the month, Oakalla's last prisoner walked down the front steps and passed through the front gate, ending the prison's seventy-nine years of service.

The official closing ceremonies were conducted on Saturday, July 13, 1991. Since controversy had marked the building of Oakalla in 1911, it didn't seem too out-of-place to have disruptions during the closing of the gaol. As a small crowd of onlookers and news reporters heard officials commemorate the historic prison, the proceedings were interrupted when Rev. Russ Manthorpe, Oakalla's long-serving Protestant Chaplain, began to speak. "Shame, Shame," yelled Native Indian Russell Kwaksistala. The protestor was demanding an apology from the Corrections Branch for incarcerating his ancestors in Oakalla in 1922, after being convicted of organizing a Potlatch. He argued that it was people like the minister who helped put natives in gaol because they wanted them to practise Christianity instead of observing their traditional Winter Ceremonies.

But for thousands of Lower Mainland citizens, Oakalla's closing was very much an upbeat event. Elwood Veitch, Burnaby's local MLA, had been pressing for the prison's closure for many years. He felt that local residents were due for a party, since they had had to "suffer with this facility for so long." In conjunction with the Burnaby Hospital Foundation, a celebration was planned for the closing weekend. The "Jail House Rock" was an evening of dinner, live theatre, and dance. The following day was "Escape to Oakalla," where the prison was transformed into a carnival with three entertainment stages, clowns, concession stands, tours of the prison, and even authentic Oakalla bricks for sale. During the weekend an estimated 15,000 people came to the prison, raising thousands of dollars towards the purchase of new medical equipment for Burnaby Hospital. The sounds of children playing and people singing were a sharp contrast to the violent screams of rioting inmates only a few months before.

The Corrections Branch opened the prison to the public for two weeks following the closing ceremonies to allow one final glimpse of an era long past. The self-guiding tour displayed the boarded-up gallows, Death Row, and the site of the New Year's Day mass escape from beneath the Cow Barn. On display in the Officers' Canteen were inmate paintings, prison memorabilia, and a cabinet full of weapons and other contraband that had been seized over the years. Although the public now had an opportunity to see the conditions that guards and inmates had worked and lived in, they would never experience the ever-present tension that once existed within its walls.

Eight Decades of Service
When the prison was built in 1912, it was a model for Corrections throughout North America. Forty years later, it had deteriorated to one of the nation's worst. Hugh Christie took the bull by the horns, and in just five years, reclaimed Oakalla as one of the top prisons in Canada. However, following his departure, it regressed, and with each passing year became more overcrowded, outdated, and violent.

During its final decade, Oakalla was called an "eye-sore" and something that "belongs in the Dark Ages." Even though it was criticized by many, and the majority of their complaints were well-founded, it would be unfortunate to jump to the conclusion that the prison had served no benefit to the community or that it had always been a "sordid, grubby, miserable, hopeless mess."[2] Oakalla served British Columbians by keeping thousands of dangerous prisoners out of the community, and while this book relates a number of high-profile escapes, the majority of those who forcefully found their freedom were low security-risk inmates. Oakalla also acted as the "last resort" for other institutions which could not cope with their most dangerous offenders. Moreover, up until the late 1960s Oakalla was the largest employer in Burnaby, providing an unforgettable career for countless men and women, even though it was a thankless, and often dangerous, job.

In retrospect, for many years Oakalla was a violent, noisy, and overcrowded institution. It was often rumoured that criminals facing sentences around the two-year mark would opt for federal time rather than risk being sent to Oakalla. Even though discipline was not as strict in later years as it had been in the early 1900s, Oakalla's tense atmosphere always made it a hard place to "do time." Looking at the other side of the coin, the wardens and staff faced formidable hurdles in trying to maintain an orderly institution with such a wide variety of prisoners crammed into small and outdated living spaces. By and large, these men and women dedicated nearly eighty years of service trying to make the best out of a prison that held some of this country's worst.

In 1992 a wrecking ball began to demolish Oakalla.

Epilogue

In early 1992, a wrecking ball began demolishing Oakalla to make way for a mixture of housing and parkland. Over 500 prime real-estate townhouses and apartments will be built on the south side of Deer Lake, with a majestic view of the North Shore's snow-capped mountains. From the sale of the lands, the provincial government agreed to donate $1 million towards the environmental clean-up of polluted Deer Lake.

In March 1993, the first lots on Oakalla's old site were sold to Polygon Development Ltd. for $12.5 million. Today Oakalla is just a memory with no physical structures remaining to remind us of Burnaby's historic prison.

Appendix A
Executions at Oakalla

Number	Name	Age	Date
2883	IGNACE, Alec	25	1919-08-29
4905	ROBINSON, Alan	20	1922-07-28
5080	PAULSON, Alex	25	1922-07-28
8063	BOW, Chong Sam	45	1925-01-15
9997	BAKER, Owen B.	39	1926-01-14
10048	MYERS, Harry F.	24	1926-01-14
11191	DeBORTILI, Alexander	40	1926-07-14
10996	PASQUALI, Benito	50	1926-07-14
12726	BAILEY, Kenneth R.	25	1928-01-09
12901	YAOKI, Nichi	32	1928-01-09
14464	NASSA, Dominico	25	1929-07-23
20129	SOWRY, Mike	52	1931-08-14
20926	MATHOFF, Bill	40	1931-09-04
20709	SAKURADA, Suikichi	40	1931-12-30
20710	HITOMI, Tadao'	50	1931-12-30
27947	GEORGE, Richardson	32	1936-11-06
27948	GEORGE, Eneas	39	1936-11-06
31011	RUSSELL, Charles	27	1936-11-06
31113	DUNBAR, Earl	32	1936-11-27
31651	MACCHIONE, Vincent	36	1938-08-26
38535	WRIGHT, R. A.	68	1939-06-16
42111	SYLVESTER, Frank	21	1941-01-24
45831	BEATTY, Douglas R.	27	1941-11-22
49857	HAINEN, William J.	29	1945-10-20
47985	PRINCE, Alex	23	1945-11-28
50281	POTTER, Byron	49	1946-01-10
52917	HOUSTON, Davis	28	1947-10-01
53709	MEDOS, Harry	19	1947-10-01
60671	PRESTYKO, Walter	34	1950-02-28
60716	WOROBEC, William J.	37	1950-02-28
62775	DUCHARME, Frederick R.	33	1950-07-14
62573	OULETTE, Joseph A.	21	1951-05-29
69658	DAVIDOFF, John K.	48	1951-12-11
71447	CUNNINGHAM, Arthur B.	60	1952-08-05
73937	VIATKIN, Alexander	24	1953-01-20
78020	MATHEWS, Charles	21	1953-11-10
86060	BORDENIUK, Peter	60	1955-03-29
87290	HOODLEY, Robert	21	1955-05-17
81746	VINCENT, Lawrence	27	1955-06-14
91238	GRAHAM, Robert	24	1956-05-22
98129	BUCK, Evan G.	29	1957-02-19
92224	GORDON, Joe	36	1957-04-02
94839	EATON, Gerald	51	1957-07-16
117913	MANTHA, Leo	33	1959-04-28

Appendix B
Escapes From Oakalla 1940-1990

Year	Escapes	Year	Escapes
1939/40	8	1965/66	15
1940/41	8	1966/67	22
1941/42	11	1967/68	23
1942/43	16	1968/69	19
1943/44	10	1969/70	12
1944/45	2	1970/71	12
1945/46	5	1971/72	17
1946/47	6	1972/73	14
1947/48	18	1973/74	26
1948/49	16	1975	20
1949/50	4	1976	35
1950/51	8	1977	34
1951/52	15	1978	32
1952/53	14	1979	16
1953/54	12	1980/81	30
1954/55	12	1981/82	27
1955/56	7	1982/83	19
1956/57	27	1983/84	32
1957/58	10	1984/85	22
1958/59	24	1985/86	19
1959/60	12	1986/87	23
1960/61	37	1987/88	33
1961/62	30	1989	0
1962/63	37	1990	2
1963/64	26		
1964/65	11	**Total:**	890

Note: Yearly totals from 1940 to 1974 include all escapes from Oakalla: men, women, and young offenders. Figures from 1975 to 1990 are only male inmates who have escaped custody. The majority of above totals are based on fiscal year figures (April 1 to March 31) which have been published in Annual Reports.

Appendix C
Attempted and Successful Suicides
April 1964 to January 1968

Attempted Suicides:	391
Successful Suicides:	17

Per Year:
- 1964 - 3
- 1965 - 4
- 1966 - 6
- 1967 - 3
- 1968 - 1

Sex:

Male -	16
Female -	1

Marital Status:

Married -	2
Single -	14
Unknown -	1

Method of Injury:

Slashing	70%	(0% successful)
Hanging	29%	(12% successful)
Other (e.g. swallowing)	1%	(0% successful)
All Methods	100%	(4% successful)

Location of Suicides:

West Wing	7 (41%)
Isolation	1 (6%)
South Wing	1 (6%)
Hospital	1 (6%)
East Wing	1 (6%)
Observation	1 (6%)
Westgate	3 (17%)
Women's Gaol	1 (6%)
Trailers	1 (6%)

A summary of research data on successful and attempted suicides at Oakalla over a four-year period. Compiled by Supervisor S.A. Thorvaldson, Central Classification on Feb. 26, 1968.

Notes

Chapter One

1. "Keeping six" is prison vernacular for keeping a watch out for the guards or police.
2. "Burnaby's Protest," *The British Columbian*, 24 July 1911.
3. "Building for Prison Farm," *The British Columbian*, 4 July 1911.
4. Public Works Contract between the Honourable Thomas Taylor,(Miniter of Public Works), and Smith and Sherborne Contractors, Vancouver, October 9, 1911, Clause No. 26.
5. Diana Doherty and John W. Ekstedt, *Conflict Care and Control: The History of the Corrections Branch in British Columbia* (Burnaby: Simon Fraser University Institute For Studies in Criminal Justice Policy, 1991), p. 50.
6. The second dominant philosophy at that time was called the "Pennsylvania System": prisoners were kept in total isolation for the duration of their sentence. This had been popular in European countries.

Chapter Two

1. Michael Stone (Ed.), "Bert Price" in *Pioneer Tales of Burnaby,* (Burnaby: The Corporation of the District of Burnaby, 1987), p. 156.
2. From December 6, 1917 to March 31, 1923, Police Superintendent Colin Campbell relieved McMynn of his duties as Oakalla's warden. The reason for the administrative change is unknown; however, McMynn returned in 1923 to run the prison for another six years.
3. "Men Hanged at Oakalla," *The Province*, 28 July 1922, p. 1.
4. "Two Hijackers Hanged at Dawn; Bid Each Other Calm Farewell," *Vancouver Sun*, 14 Jan. 1926, p. 1.
5. Eric Newsome, *The Case of the Beryl G* (Victoria: Orca Book Publishers, 1989), pp. 92-93.
6. "Two Hijackers Hanged at Dawn..."
7. "'Let 'Er Go!' Says Slayer as Pair Go to Death at Oakalla," *Vancouver Sun*, 9 Jan. 1928, p. 1.

Chapter Three

1. "Pooley Doubts Oakalla Jail Charges," *Vancouver Sun*, 15 April 1930, p.2.
2. "Police Tell of Gun Duel," *Vancouver Sun*, 14 March 1931, p. 2.
3. "Government to Overhaul B.C. Prison," *The Province*, 6 Jan. 1932, p. 1

4. "Frank Sorge, Oakalla Fugitive, Recaptured by City Detectives, *Vancouver Sun,* 7 Jan. 1932, p. 1.

5. Diana Doherty and John W. Ekstedt, *Conflict Care and Control: The History of the Corrections Branch in British Columbia* (Burnaby: Simon Fraser University Institute for Studies in Criminal Justice Policy, 1991), p. 58.

6. Guy Richmond, *Prison Doctor: One Man's Story that Must be Told in Canada Today* (Surrey B.C.: Nunaga Publishings, 1975), p. 49.

7. "Death Comes to Oakalla Once a Year; Visit of One Man Puts Pall Over Prison," *The Province,* 17 Sept. 1948, p. 21.

8. "Oakalla Prison Going Out in Style," *Vancouver Sun,* 5 July 1991, p.A1.

9. "Oakalla Gaol," *The Province,* 27 Nov. 1937, p. 1.

10. "'Take Care of My Horse' Doomed Man's Last Request," T*he Province,* 24 Jan. 1941, p. 12.

Chapter Four

1. "Suitcasing" refers to a method of smuggling, more commonly employed by female visitors, who place the contraband (i.e. drugs) into a rubber receptacle (balloon or condom) and then insert it into a bodily orifice. Once inside the prison, the smuggler retrieves the drugs and passes it to the prisoner who conceals it in his mouth, or swallows it and recovers it at a later time.

2. "Death Comes to Oakalla Once a Year; Visit of One Man Puts Pall Over Prison," *The Province,* 17 Sept. 1948, p. 21.

3. "It's a Grim Job Hangman Admits," The Province, 24 Feb. 1950, p. 1.

4. Ibid.

5. "'Full Enquiry' Into Oakalla Beheading," *The Province,* 14 Jan. 1946, p. 1.

6. "'Shot Me As I Fell,' Says Det. Hoare," *Vancouver Sun,* 27 Feb. 1947, p. 9. Due to an inexplicable oversight by the Vancouver Police Department, it wasn't until 1992, well into his retirement, before Percy Hoare received a Chief's commendation for his heroic efforts.

7. "30 Windows Broken in Oakalla Flare-up," *Vancouver Sun,* 1 March, 1948, p. 1.

8. Ibid. It is not known on what basis the reporter came to this conclusion.

9. "'I Want to See Him Hang' Slayer's Last Request," *The Province,* 28 Feb. 1950, p. 1.

10. "'Distasteful' Stories Bring Ban on Press at Hangings," *Vancouver Sun,* 17 March 1950, p. 30.

11. "Ducharme Calm at Trial Ordeal," *Vancouver Sun,* 11 Mar.,1950, p. 2.

12. Jack Webster, *Webster! An Autobiography by Jack Webster* (Vancouver: Douglas and McIntyre, 1990), p. 40.

13. "Court Hears Dramatic Letter From Ducharme," *Vancouver Sun*, 14 March 1950, p. 2.

14. E. Pepler, C.W. Topping and E.G.B. Stevens (Commissioners), *Report of the Commission Appointed by the Attorney-General to Inquire Into the State and Management of the Gaols of British Columbia* (Victoria: Kings Printer, 1951), p. 5.

15. D.J. MacNamara, "The Medical Model in Corrections," *Criminology*, 14 (February 1977), 439-40.

16. Pepler, Topping, and Stevens, pp. 17-19.

Chapter Five

1. "Hugh Christie Named Warden at Oakalla," *Vancouver Sun*, 25 June 1952, p. 1.

2. "Warden Forecast Oakalla Prison Riot," *The Province*, 3 Oct. 1952, p. 1.

3. "Swift Punishment Meted Out to Oakalla Mutineers," *Vancouver Sun*, 3 Oct. 1952, p. 2.

4. Hugh Christie, *Memorandum - Re: Riot - Oakalla Gaol, October 2, 1952* (3 October 1952), p. 2.

5. "Swift Punishment Meted Out to Oakalla Mutineers."

6. Ibid.

7. Christie, p. 5.

8. "Oakalla Becoming One of Canada's Top Jails," *Vancouver Sun*, 29 April 1955, p. 6.

9. *Annual Report of the Director of Correction, 1966/67* (Victoria: Attorney-General's Department, 1968), p. 38.

10. *Annual Report of the Director of Correction, 1953/54,* (Victoria: Attorney-General's Department, 1955), p. 19.

11. "Oakalla Becoming One of Canada's Top Jails."

12. "Prison Warden Explains Stand Against Hanging, *Victoria Daily Times*, 29 April 1955, p. 3.

13. "Slayer Hanged at Oakalla," *Vancouver Sun*, 5 Aug. 1952, p. 2.

14. "Viatkin, Slayer, Hanged at Oakalla, *Vancouver Sun*, 20 Jan. 1953, p. 7.

15. "Brazen Ruse Frees Convict," *Vancouver Sun*, 21 March 1955, p. 1.

16. "Slayer Battles Hangman With Fists, Feet, Tongue," *Vancouver Sun*, 14 June 1955, p. 3.

17. Ibid.

18. "Jail Guard Freed After Ordeal," *Vancouver Sun*, 8 May 1956, p. 1.

19. Ibid., p. C3.
20. "'Routine' Oakalla Day Ends Up in Nightmare," *The Province,* 7 May 1956, p. 21.
21. Dr. Richmond's personal account of this ordeal is related in his autobiography: Richmond, Guy. *Prison Doctor: One Man's Story that Must be Told in Canada Today.* Surrey, B.C.: Nunaga Publishing, 1975.
22. "Oakalla's 'Six Hours of Deadly Threat' as Inmates Hold Guard Hostage," *The Province,* 8 May 1956, p. 9.
23. Ibid.
24. "Joe Gordon Hanged With Sneer for 'Stool Pigeon'," *Vancouver Sun,* 2 April 1957, p. 15.
25. *Annual Report of the Director of Correction 1962/63* (Victoria: Attorney General's Department, 1964), p. 22.

Chapter Six

1. W.H. Mulligan, *Memorandum - Re: Recent Disturbances and Remand Facilities Oakalla Prison Farm* (25 May 1964), p. 3.
2. Ibid., p. 4.
3. "Cell Suicides Spark Hysteria," *Vancouver Sun,* 20 Sept. 1966, p. 1.
4. "Oakalla looking for Psychiatrist," *The Province,* 23 Sept. 1966, p. 1.
5. *Corrections Branch Annual Report 1972/73* (Victoria: British Columbia Corrections Branch, 1974), p. 13.
6. W.H. Mulligan, *Report - Escape: Inmate Clarke... Inmate McCann... And Assault on Correctional Officer T.A. Harris* (25 Oct. 1966), p. 1.
7. This officer, Rene Gobillot, later became Oakalla's eighth warden.
8. W.H. Mulligan, *Memorandum - Re: Escape - Bird, Turner, and West - March 9, 1967* (13 March 1967), pp. 2-3.
9. "Last of Three Prison Breakers Surrenders to Sun Reporter," *Vancouver Sun,* 9 March 1967, p. 1.
10. "Cool Mom had Code," *The Province,* 10 March 1967, p. 1.
11. "Fleeing Prisoner Shot by Guard," *Vancouver Sun,* 16 April 1968, p. 1.
12. "Police Capture Four Escapees," *Vancouver Sun,* 7 October 1968, p. 2.
13. W. H. Mulligan, *Memorandum - Re: O.P.F. No. 221826... Jaspert* (5 August 1969), p. 2
14. "Prison Guard Wounded," *The Province,* 17 March 1969, p. 10.
15. *Memorandum - Re: O.P.F. No. 221826... Jaspert,* p. 5.
16. Due to the confidential nature of this incident, the identities of the

officer and inmate involved have been substituted with the fictitious names "Collins" and "Beaupre."

17. W. H. Mulligan, *Memorandum - Confidential Report - Threat on Life of Security Officer... by O.P.F. No. 222590...*, p. 1.
18. "Yippies Plan War Paint for Oakalla Be-Out," *Vancouver Sun*, 9 July 1970, p. 62.
19. W.H. Mulligan, *Memorandum - Re: Annual Report - Lower Mainland Regional Correctional Centre (1970/71)*, p. 13.

Chapter Seven

1. *Corrections Branch Annual Report 1971/72*, British Columbia Corrections Branch (Victoria: Queen's Printer, 1973), p. 49.
2. "Murder Suspect Found Hanging in Oakalla Cell," *The Province*, 8 May 1975, p. 29.
3. Murder Suspect Hangs Herself," *The Province*, 5 Sept. 1975, p. 21.
4. "Sex Conduct to be Probed," *Vancouver Sun*, 25 Oct. 1977, p. A1.
5. "Inside 'Hotel Oakalla' - Sex, Intrigue," *Vancouver Sun*, 19 Nov. 1977, p. A1. Surprisingly, this allegation was never investigated by the Royal Commission.
6. Madam Justice Patricia Proudfoot (Commissioner), *Report of the British Columbia Royal Commission on the Incarceration of Female Offenders* (Victoria: Queen's Printer, 1978), p. 19.
7. Ibid., pp. 19-22.
8. Ibid., p. 24.
9. Ibid., p. 25.
10. "Woman Hostage Aided by Age," *Vancouver Express*, 29 Dec. 1978, p. 1.
11. "Female Prisoners at Oakalla Stage Cow Barn Sit-in," *Vancouver Sun*, 7 Jan. 1980, p. A3.
12. T. Webb (Summarized for H.B. Bjarnason) *Chronological Sequence of Events - Disturbances LMRCC* (February 1980), p. 1.
13. "Catch 22 in Prison Riot," *The Province*, 10 Feb. 1980, p. A7
14. "Prisoners Returned to Cells After Smash-up at Oakalla," *Vancouver Sun*, 15 Feb. 1980, p. A12.
15. H.B. Bjarnason, *Memorandum - Re: Attempted Escape and Disturbance - South Wing - July 7, 1980* (24 July 1980), p. 1.
16. "Olson Fears for his Safety," *Vancouver Sun*, 25 Sept. 1981, p. 1.
17. H.B. Bjarnason, *Memorandum - Re: Sit-in and Disturbance - South and East Wings, LMRCC, September 19 and 20, 1982* (27 Sept. 1982), p. 1.
18. *Report on the Riot at LMRCC on November 22, 1983*, Ministry of Attorney-General, Corrections Branch: Prepared by Inspection and

Standards Division (23 Dec. 1983), p. 15.

19. Ibid. p. 1.
20. "Damage Set at $150,000: Prison Riot Probed," *Vancouver Sun,* 24 Nov. 1983, p. A1.
21. *Report on the Riot at LMRCC on November 22, 1983,* p. 3.
22. Ibid., p. 5.
23. Ibid., p. 12.
24. Several years earlier, a private food services company had taken over meal preparation at Oakalla, thus all employees in the Kitchen were civilians, and there was no need to lock the back door.

Chapter Eight

1. Interview with Corrections Officer P. Kitto, 1991.
2. Ibid. (Inmate Dean claimed that when the handcuffs were removed, Officer Kitto punched him first and he struck back to protect himself.)
3. Ian L. Drost (Commissioner), *Royal Commission Report Into the Escape From LMRCC on January 1, 1988* (Victoria: Queen's Printer, 1988), p. 22.
4. Ibid., p. 28.
5. Ibid., p. 43.
6. Ibid., p. 44.
7. Ibid., p. 45.
8. Ibid., p. 46.
9. "Inmate 'socked' it to 'em," *The Province,* 6 Jan., 1988, p. 5.
10. Drost, pp. 50-51.
11. Interview with Corrections Officer J. Bainas, 1991.
12. The tactical team had been on duty New Year's Eve with the members stationed in the Officer's Lounge, ready to immediately deal with any disturbances in the Main Gaol.
13. Courtesy BCTV, January 2, 1988. Hall's allegations were dismissed at the Inquiry.
14. Drost, pp. 58-59.

Chapter Nine

1. "B.C.'s High-Tech Jail Without Bars," *The Province,* 26 June 1990, p. 14.
2. Claire Culhane, *Barred From Prison* (Vancouver: Pulp Press, 1979).

Photo Credits

Illustration

Bibliography

Andersen, Earl, Martin Hole, and Elinor Stock. *A Short History of Oakalla: 1912-1991.* Co-ordinated by the British Columbia Corrections Branch History Committee, 1991.

Christie, Hugh. *Administrative Structure and Process Within a Penal Institution.* Vancouver: University of British Columbia (MSW) Thesis, 1952.

Culhane, Claire. *Barred from Prison.* Vancouver: Pulp Press, 1979

Culhane, Claire. *Still Barred from Prison.* Montreal: Black Rose Books, 1985.

Doherty, Diana, and John W. Ekstedt. *Conflict Care and Control: The History of the Corrections Branch in British Columbia.* Burnaby, B.C.: Simon Fraser University Institute For Studies In Criminal Justice Policy, 1991

Drost, Ian L.(Commissioner) *Royal Commission Report Into the Escape From LMRCC on January 1, 1988.* Victoria, B.C.: Queen's Printer, 1988

MacNamara, D.J. "The Medical Model of Corrections." *Criminology,* 14 (February 1977), 439-440.

Pepler, E., C.W. Topping, and E.G.B. Stevens (Commissioners). *Report to the Honourable Gordon S. Wismer, K.C., Attorney-General of British Columbia, on the State and Management of the Gaols of the Province.* Victoria, B.C.: King's Printer, 1950.

Proudfoot, Patricia M. (Commissioner). *Report of the British Columbia Royal Commission on the Incarceration of Female Offenders.* Victoria, B.C.: Queen's Printer, 1978.

Richmond, Dr. Guy. *Prison Doctor: One Man's Story that Must be Told in Canada Today.* Surrey, B.C.: Nunaga Publishings, 1975.

Richmond, Dr. Guy. *Shadows of a Violent Mind.* Surrey, B.C.: Antonson Publishing, 1978.

Schroeder, Andreas. *Shaking it Rough: A Prison Memoir.* Toronto: Doubleday Cananda, 1976.

Scott, Jack David. *Four Walls in the West: The Story of the British Columbia Penitentiary.* New Westminster: Retired Federal Prison Officers' Association of B.C., 1984.

Stone, Michael (Editor). *Pioneer Tales of Burnaby.* Burnaby, B.C.: The Corporation of the District of Burnaby, 1987.

Swan, Joe. *A Century of Service: The Vancouver Police 1886-1986.* Vancouver: Vancouver Police Historical Society and Centennial Museum, 1986.

Webster, Jack. *Webster! An Autobiography by Jack Webster.* Vancouver: Douglas and McIntyre, 1990.

Annual Reports:

Annual Report of the Inspector of Gaols. Victoria: Attorney General's Department, 1934-1958.

Annual Report of the Director of Correction. Victoria: Attorney General's Department, 1959-1970.

Corrections Branch Annual Report. Victoria: British Columbia Corrections Branch, 1971-1990.

Unpublished Corrections Branch Reports:

Bjarnason, H.B. *Memorandum - Re: Annual Report - Lower Mainland Regional Correctional Centre (1975).*

Bjarnason, H.B. *Memorandum - Re: Annual Report - Lower Mainland Regional Correctional Centre (1976).*

Bjarnason, H.B. *Memorandum - Re: Annual Report - Oakalla District, Fiscal Year Ending March 31, 1983.*

Bjarnason, H.B. *Memorandum - Re: Attempted Escape and Disturbance - South Wing - July 7, 1980.* (24 July 1980)

Bjarnason, H.B. *Memorandum - Re: Sit-In and Disturbance - South and East Wings, LMRCC, September 19 and 20, 1982.* (27 Sept. 1982).

Christie, Hugh. *Memorandum - Re: Riot - Oakalla Gaol, October 2, 1952* (3 October 1952).

Linn, L.C. *Report: Disturbance and Events Leading Thereto, Women's Unit Lower Mainland Regional Correctional Centre, Sunday, April 7, 1974.*

Mulligan, W.H. *Memorandum - Confidential Report - Threat on Life of Security Officer... By O.P.F. No. 222590...*

Mulligan, W.H. *Memorandum - Re: Annual Report - Lower Mainland Regional Correctional Centre (1970/71).*

Mulligan, W.H. *Memorandum - Re: Annual Report - Lower Mainland Regional Correctional Centre (1972/73).*

Mulligan, W.H. *Memorandum - Re: Annual Report - Lower Mainland Regional Correctional Centre (1973/74).*

Mulligan, W.H. *Memorandum - Re: Assault on Security Officer G.E. Terry.* (25 June 1968).

Mulligan, W.H. *Memorandum - Re: Escape - Inmates Bird, Turner, and West - March 9, 1967.* (13 March 1967).

Mulligan, W.H. *Memorandum - O.P.F. No. 221826 - ... Jaspert* (5 August 1969).

Mulligan, W.H. *Memorandum - Re: Recent Disturbances and Remand Facilities Oakalla Prison Farm.* (25 May 1964).

Mulligan, W.H. *Report - Escape: Inmate Clarke... Inmate McCann... And Assault on Correctional Officer T.A. Harris.* (25 Oct. 1966).

Report on the Riot at LMRCC on November 22, 1983. Ministry of Attorney-General, Corrections Branch: Prepared by Inspection and

Standards Division (23 Dec. 1983).

Tabin, T. *Memorandum - Re: East Wing Disturbance September 19, 1982.* (23 Sept. 1982).

Webb, T. (Summarized for H.B. Bjarnason) *Chronological Sequence of Events - Disturbance LMRCC.* (February 1980).

Index

Turner, Inmate, 108-111
Turpin, Dr., 99.

U

U.S. Bureau of Narcotics, 76.
Uncles, Officer, 108-111.

V

Vancouver General Hospital, 27, 41,
53, 90, 91, 112, 115, 139.
Vancouver Liberation Front, 119.
Vancouver Police, 21, 51-53, 90-93,
111.
Vancouver Pre-trial Services Cen-
tre, 125, 139.
Veitch, Elwood, 170.
Viatkin, Alexander, 75.
Vincent, Lawrence, 78-79.

W

Walker, Donald, 55.
Walla Walla Penitentiary, 128.
Wanless, Elsie, 128-129.
Washington State Police, 37.
Waslyenchuk, John, 77, 80-83.
Wasson, Officer, 140.
Weber, Mrs., 110-111.
Webster, Jack, 126.
West, Inmate, 108-111.
White, Inmate, 159-161, 166.
Wilcox, Ellis, 31-35.
Williams, Inmate, 161.
Worobec, William, 57-58.
Wright, R. A., 50.

Y

Yaoki, Nichi, 27.
Yippies, 119-120.
Young Offenders, 54-56, 61.

Z

Zoltan Kiss Architects, 168.